AF488523

PRAISES

Mahatma Gandhi said, "Be the change you want to see in the world." Thus, far in my life, I have met many inspirational people, Nobel laureates, mentors, etc. But no one other than Dr. Vaishalli is more befitting of this quote. All of us have, at some point, been to a doctor who simply treats the symptoms. Today, very few doctors take the time to treat the root of the disease, especially mental illness. Being the one who knows Dr. Vaishalli as a friend, my yoga teacher and my mentor; I know that she goes above and beyond the call of duty. Right from gaining expertise in psychology to naturopathy and lately Pranic Healing; I have seen Dr. Vaishalli learning relentlessly and integrating all her learning in her practice. In my opinion, this book is an outcome-driven guide that will help you navigate through testing times with brimming mental and physical strength. I would also quote; this book is a super-highway to discover your best SELF.

Amriti Lulla
Ph.D. (Molecular Medicine)

I recently had the good fortune of reading your book Midlife Marvels. It is great! Phenomenal! Superb! It has been well-written, it contains sound and practical steps to transpire the Midlife Magic. In fact, I have already benefited from our discussions on this, which I will remember for years to come. You have a beautiful mind and I wish I could write like you.

Ganesh Pendhari
Faculty @ AOL & Yoga Practitioner

I must say that you have chosen a perfect topic as each individual goes through a midlife crisis whatever may be the cause. Being my doctor and my mentor, each time I visit you, your unique ways of treatments (not to forget that your clinic being my confession room) has not only healed me physically but always made me emotionally strong. Thank you for helping my students, your guidance has helped them win medals.

YashrajTarkar
Indian National Coach for Lifesaving Sports

Congratulations!
There is a science behind how depression works and you have rightly picked the topic that shines the torch on this subject.

Your book reflects deep knowledge and represents the positive side of life.

Satyajeet and Nalini
Project Onshore Engineering and IT Management

This book is a **One-Stop Destination** to amplify your Understanding, Dealing, Managing, Curing, Healing. This book is the master key to deal with the Big Entity named **Depression** through various modes, channels and procedures. I would say it's a Gift to millions of people in the world who are in the chasm of Depression.

Shailendra Hanumante
Founder & CEO Desibol InfoTech Solutions

Dr. Vaishalli, an Alternative and Holistic therapist with excellent credentials, has dedicated almost two decades to the study and healing of midlife depression. This self-help approach will help millions going through a crisis, in resolving the issues rapidly and easily.

Anuradha Nittur
Pranic Healing Practitioner, Freelancer,
Writer and Researcher

Midlife Marvels

Midlife MARVELS

A SELF-HELP BOOK TO TRANSFORM
AND TRANSMUTE MIDLIFE
DEPRESSION THE HOLISTIC WAY

Authored by

Dr. Vaishalli Khangtey

MIDLIFE MARVELS

First Edition 2020

ISBN: 9798555709547

Published by Happy Self Publishing
Website: www.happyselfpublishing.com

DEDICATION

This book is dedicated to my

Guru Master Choa Kok Sui

Guru Dyannathji Ranade

And

My Beloved Parents

CONTENTS

ABOUT THE AUTHOR

Equipped with 25 years of professional experience (at the time of writing this book), Dr. Vaishalli has several accomplishments to her name. With her solution-oriented and most importantly, organic approach, she has not only healed but also enriched numerous lives on this big blue marble.

According to Dr. Vaishalli, learning is a lifetime phenomenon; 'ceasing to learn is ceasing to grow'. Therefore, the golden feathers of qualifications that she has added to her hat are myriad. Here are some of her credentials:

- **BHMS**
- **CCH (Child Health)**
- **CGO (Gynaecology and Obstetrics)**
- **CSD (Skin Diseases)**
- **MD (ALTERNATIVE MEDICINE)**
- **DIPLOMA IN YOGA**
- **PGDPC (POSTGRADUATE DIPLOMA IN PSYCHO-LOGICAL COUNSELING)**
- **And more…**

Professionally and Passionately, she works as a:

- **HOMEOPATH**
- **PRANIC HEALER/TRAINER**

- **AURA, CELLULAR AND CRYSTAL HEALER**
- **NATUROPATHIST**
- **YOGA PRACTITIONER**
- **HOLISTIC HEALING COACH**
- **PSYCHOLOGICAL COUNSELOR**
- **HYPNOTHERAPIST**
- **NUTRITIONAL DIETICIAN**

She believes that 'no one size fits all'; similarly, there is no one therapy or medication that can heal anyone and everyone. Therefore, she bolsters the ideology of offering a tailor-based solution, which has fetched miraculous results.

Besides, she has had been working with several NGO groups like Human Organization for Pioneering in Education, Bapu Trust. She has also been working with HHF (Hahnemannian Homoeopathy Forum), Pune as a trustee for 12 years. She has been researching the APPLICATION OF MIND IN HOMOEOPATHY.

She conducts seminars, gives lectures, holds counseling sessions, camps on health-related issues along with medications, etc. She also carries out free online meditations and orientation sessions on Pranic Healing, Homeopathy Consultation and Treatment regularly. Her Pranic Healing workshops are said to be a real treat for soul and health.

She has been felicitated by many local groups/organizations for her outstanding charitable work in her field. She, along with her colleagues, organizes regular free feeding programs under the project of FOOD FOR HUNGRY wherein the team distributes clothes, grains, etc. to the needy people in and around Pune.

Lately, she has been invited as the chief guest on many affluent platforms.

During her professional journey, she has been accoladed with numerous awards and appreciations. Recently, in 2020, she received the Punyadham Award for the virtuous contributions to the Pune city

She has assigned herself a mission to *help the masses by spreading the importance of living a balanced physical and mental life*. These two aspects majorly form the basis of our life, whether we will live a suffocated life or with a smile at every mile. However, as they say, awareness is the first step to change. So, to spread mindfulness, she keeps inking articles on health care that have been published in various newspapers and magazines. And this book is a giant leap in the pursuit of this mission of hers.

PREFACE

Medical practice has undergone an enormous change over the past three decades. Our knowledge of the causes of various illnesses has flourished tremendously along with the depth of the cellular and molecular architecture of our various organs including the brain. However, with the yardstick of these progressive developments, have we been able to treat ailments more effectively? The answer to this is *Yes and No*. Undoubtedly, technical advancements have been the real marvels for treating many diseases. But there are still manifold mental and emotional diseases that are yet to be treated with equal satisfaction.

In the light of my practical experience of more than 3 decades, there have been ample cases that have taught me '*we cannot understand the disease unless we understand the person who has the disease*'.

Dr. Vaishalli Khangtey is a very dedicated practitioner who has always been an innovative path-finder. She has compiled her immense experience in this marvelous book in a very concise manner. The book has been orchestrated in a way that a common man, as well as a medical practitioner, can understand. You will find practical and result-driven alternatives to manage depression of mild to a moderate degree which can be called self-healing. The inner peace acquired through Dr. Vaishalli's shared techniques on a psycho-spiritual level is the gateway to self-healing.

My Best Wishes to Dr. Vaishalli for writing such an exclusive book on alternative therapies for Mid-life Depression as there is a dearth of such easy-to-understand books today.

Dr. Bipin Deshpande,
Dermatologist
Fellow, American Academy of Dermatology

FOREWORD

These are the times when experts from all fields should share their skillset and experiences with the common man in the means and language understandable by everyone. People need help and they seek it from anyone willing to help. But some can get fooled and misdirected.

Seldom do we meet and read articles, letters from experts who can translate their thoughts, technicalities and knowledge into simple, layman's terms.

Dr. Vaishalli is one such expert who gained a lot of first-hand experience in treating people on their physical, mental and energetic levels. She is a trusted friend with whom you can share your pain, while she tactfully uses all her skills to drive greater healing results. This book is the nectar of her years of learning and interactions with clients/patients in her clinic in Pune and other places.

"It takes a good effort to learn something.
It takes a lot more effort to put that learning into practice.
It takes a greater effort to master the arts and skills of the sciences you know.
It takes even more effort to ingrain all of that in a book."

FOREWORD

This book is a handy, easy-reference for "Do It Your-self" (DIY) shared by Dr. Vaishalli. The world needs such books inked by experts and specialists who can synchronize simple means of self-care or self-help so that the ones who are suffering can now bring their search to a screeching halt.

I am sure the readers will gain a lot of inspiration and joy while they scroll through the pages of this book. I also wish the author lots of success and blessings to continue the good work she has undertaken.

Dr. Prashant M.D, B.A
Musician, Teacher, Healer
State of Maryland

INTRODUCTION

Before I take you on this journey, let me declare a gospel truth. We might have heard this for a number of times but unfortunately, we keep heading in the opposite direction. Hence, this truth lays buried under tons of soil as we are on a self-denial trip. And the truth is; *we all are destined to live a happy life; come high water or tide*. We all have been installed with a software called 'happiness forever' which will get reactivated after you complete this book. But somehow, we have quarantined the software by installing several other malicious software starting from stress, anxiety, fear, worry, pain, phobia leading to depression and many such menacing Trojans.

Therefore, the first step to break free of all such cobwebs is self-awareness; 'awareness is the first step to massive change'. So, how to be self-aware? How to litmus test if you are victim to any of these modern-life bugs?

Well, you do not have to go through a scanning machine or some tests; all the answers lie within you! Let me ask you a few more questions:

- Do you wake up with curious and energetic eyes, or is it yet another morning?
- Do you sometimes or usually feel a gush of emotions or distress without any reason?

- Do you feel that your midlife journey lacks enthusiasm and you hit a blind wall most of the time?
- Do you sometimes or usually find unnecessary stress taking a toll on you?
- Even during the happy moments, do you sometimes/usually find yourself enveloped in fear of the unknown?
- Have you been struggling at the emotional (mental) or physical (health) front?
- Last but not least, when was the last time you laughed your heart out?

What if, I say, I can help you come out of this abyss. Does it sound good or does this enthuse you in some way? Believe it or not but it is true! I really want to help you.

According to WHO, globally more than 264 million people of all ages suffer from depression and all the more in midlife as life takes a different turn altogether.

These alarming statistics ring an alarm in every affected ear. It is quite unfortunate that we usually find ourselves like a spineless wanderer lost in this fair of the world. Believe it or not, midlife is like a Herculean task and we, with our own limited knowledge, try to tackle it. But alas, if you neglect it, suppress it, do not share with anyone or not seek the help, you will not realize when you slipped into this dark grey area. Gradually, you will find yourself becoming a permanent resident of this darksome zone. This is the zone that reads 'depression' but we fail to read the signboard.

Depression is a very big entity (not trying to scare you; making you aware of the reality) but ironically, we often use this word too casually and at times, even pridefully. Sometimes we are in such a fix that we are unable to understand ourselves as it might start with simple anxiety.

And till we really understand as to what exactly we are going through, we have already entered the territory of depression.

But here's the good news. If you start being aware of your altered thoughts and emotions and start taking charge of yourself by working it out, you can come out of it easily. So, in this book, I have tried to compile and cater to solutions. These are the solutions that if followed properly, regularly and religiously, will help you come out of midlife depression drastically.

This book is about the tried and tested solutions in my clinic which are natural and can be practiced daily. Most of them are DIY (Do It Yourself) techniques and for some, you need to see the subject expert. This book is for the millions of people who go through minor and major emotional upheavals and are trying to find solutions. As it is a completely holistic approach, you can use the techniques even if you have no support from your family or loved ones. You will find diverse workable solutions as you tread through the journey of this book. It is just like a buffet spread on the table. You can pick and choose whatever resonates with you.

Before I share more about this book, let me quickly walk you through my journey; what made me choose this profession as my passion.

Since my teens, I have seen my friends, my near and dear ones confiding in me and most of the time, when I tried to explain or give advice or solutions to their problems, they would adopt the solutions. Later, I realized that I have a good ear, I learned about my ability to listen to people and give them solutions. This helped me in my practice as a Doctor especially being a Homoeopath.

I started practicing the Applied Mind method wherein the first step is to understand the mind of the patient. The second step is the adaptation of the patient during the spell of a certain illness or disease, be it mental or physical. There could also be a certain phase in life when he or she is in dis-ease i.e. not-at-ease state. I further went on to learn Alternative medicine and got an MD degree, this again helped me extensively in my practice. I was already counseling my patients at my level, however, I felt the strong urge to boost my knowledge. Therefore, I decided to learn the nuts and bolts of counseling skills so that I could communicate more effectively with my patients. Hence, I complemented my previous degrees with another one in Psychological Counseling (PGDPC). Along with that I also learnt Yoga Therapy by pursuing a Diploma in Yoga.

With all these qualifications, little had I realized what was in store for me ahead. With all this knowledge of different therapies, just like a bouquet of roses in my vase, I started applying them to my patients. I framed tailor-made treatments for different types of diseases/problems/symptoms/ages. I was thoroughly enjoying this newfound approach as I had a unique way of treating patients. I was helping people with all kinds of therapies in my practice and then I came across Pranic Healing which is a form of energy healing. Seeing the amazing results of this method, I learnt Pranic Healing too which includes aura healing, chakra healing, cellular healing, crystal healing and much more. I added this therapy too to my bouquet. At present, I heal all kinds of patients with these different therapies that I provide under one umbrella.

My quest to learn fueled me and I went ahead to become a Pranic Healing Trainer as well. I felt this healing therapy is so amazing that it should reach the masses and benefit them in their walks of life. Hence, I conduct workshops of Pranic Healing which is a no-touch, no-drug and energy-based healing method. All these degrees and knowledge have helped me in my practice to actually heal people physically as well as mentally especially where modern medicine is not able to give complete solace to the patient. These therapies not only help exceptionally but can also be combined with other streams of medicine and heal the patient.

Nowadays, I see more patients with psychological problems rather than physical diseases. A significant number of people have an emotional/psychological background, leading them to a physical ailment especially in the midlife category. Hence, psychodynamics has become a very important part of my practice.

Being attached to an NGO (which deals with mental illnesses) as a homeopathy consultant, I see the compelling results of all the therapies which are being used at the centre. After witnessing these miraculous results in my patients, I felt that the healing and health-boosting (both physical and mental) treatments should be known to many people who can take its benefit. Therefore, I decided to move out of my limited area of work and come up with this book with only one aim in my mind; to serve the ailing at a larger level. I have been coaxed by my patients many times to pen down these results which I get in my practice so that others could benefit, but I simply ignored out of sheer laziness. However, now I feel this is the best time to come up with this book as I am celebrating the 25th year of my practice, serving the ailing ones and soothing them with these therapies.

This book starts with solutions that you may put into action as soon as you wake up in the morning and can follow throughout the day. You can choose to follow them step-by-step or in an individualized manner; whatever you like or resonates with you according to the signs and symptoms or your emotions. I have shared testimonials of my patients who have not only overcome but are completely depression-free. These testimonials can help you build your confidence; if they can, so can you.

This book helps you take baby steps and begin with your healing process. All you need to do is, read it thoroughly and then frame a plan of action thereby helping yourself reach your goal. In every treatment/solution, I have talked about the therapy, explained it with its description and procedure so that you can practice it.

I promise you that you will see fantastic results as I have seen in my clinic. I have had been treating the patients who were on the verge of slipping into depression and also those who were already into it and taking medications of antidepressants. And these procedures have driven head-turner results, most importantly, the organic way.

So why wait, grab a copy, read it thoroughly, and start taking action to see the result. If you are serious about coming out of your sufferings, go for it and experience the magic. Time is very crucial during the phase of depression. If you do not take action as soon as possible, you might not understand as to when these small signs and symptoms of anxiety, fear, worries, phobias, etc. barge you into the territory of depression.

Life is a spectacular journey. During this journey, we come across umpteen choices, to avail or to resist is completely our decision. However, there are certain choices that can prove to be life-changing. And I can assure you this book is one of such profound opportunities that can cruise you to blissful horizons.

Besides, I truly believe that you are reading this, which is a sign that the Universe has led you; to come out of your suffering. So, why wait? By reading until this page, you have already taken the first step. Now, let me hand-hold and navigate you to the life that you deserve. Let the midlife magic eventuate!

Founder of Dr. Vaishalli's Health Solutions
And The Master Care

CHAPTER 1

HOW DO WE PERCEIVE MIND AND BODY?

One Sunday evening as I was slurping my piping hot tea, my phone buzzed. Being in a relaxing mode, admiring my plants in the garden, I let it ring. After a minute or so, it rang again, so I thought I must answer the call as my profession does not allow me to avoid calls. However, till the time I edged closer to the phone, it stopped ringing. I thought its ok, I can always call later, let me savor these moments as it is quite rare that I am in such a relaxed mode. After a minute, as I took another sip, the phone rang again and now the ring was ceaseless. How could I ignore this call? I was alarmed as it is not very common for someone to keep calling me repeatedly unless there is something urgent. So, I sprinted and grabbed the phone. It was my dear friend. Before I could say hello, she uttered, "I am going to finish myself and I thought someone should know about this, hence I have called to inform you."

For some time, I couldn't understand the severity as I am in such a profession that I am used to hearing these kinds of words, day in and day out (According to my experience, I have seen that many patients who say this but do not really commit suicide, the ones who do not say usually do). But this friend of mine was an introvert. She would never let anything leak out, trying to wear a mask, showing to the world how good she is and how great her life is going. Knowing her forlong, I figured out that she was serious.

I engaged her in the conversation while I rushed to her home. The moment she saw me, she sputtered abruptly, "I am tired of life and if I had gone through all this mess at my young age, it had been still okay but now, especially in this age (37 years), I just cannot take it." She was completely torn apart because of what she was undergoing. She felt dejected in life due to betrayal, causing her to conclude her life by finishing herself. However, I tried to pacify her and asked her to elaborate over the reason. As I heard her side, I did not find any reason for her having such strong suicidal thoughts. But it is not necessary that everyone in the same situation will have the same kind of thoughts or react in the same manner. Alas, I realized she was going through a low mental state, called depression, for a long period and she never shared or confided it with anyone.

Sometimes life shows you so many different colors that you are unable to differentiate between the shades. Moreover, every individual has his or her own set of understanding about the various colors. E.g. if a painting is displayed on a wall and people are asked to opine on it, what do you think will be the opinions? I can vouch, if a hundred people see the painting, each one will have their own opinion. This depends on many aspects like how we perceive things, our personality, our past memories in context to the colors used, etc.

Depression is a common and critical problem in our life especially when it hits in our midlife. When you or your loved one is haunted by depression, life becomes a disaster. The person is unable to perform routine work and activities. Depression is a state when your self- esteem is low and you lose interest in life. At present, many people are suffering from depression and anxiety disorder but they are either unaware or rarely accept the truth and due to this, they are unable to unearth solutions at the right time. As a result, depression keeps mushrooming day-by-day and makes their life more and more taxing. If you can recognize depression on time and seek proper treatment, you can save your or someone's life.

What do people really want in life?

Most of us are like a ship in the ocean without a compass. What we want is success, satisfaction and happiness. Success is getting what you like and satisfaction is liking what you get.

Reflect on the following exchange between a traveler and a tourist guide –

TRAVELLER – What will be the weather at this point?

GUIDE – The weather is going to be what I like.

TRAVELLER – How can you get the weather you like?

GUIDE – I don't always get the weather I like. Therefore, I learn to like what I get, so I get the weather that I like.

> "The art of getting what I like and liking what I get
> should be cultivated by everyone."
> - UNKNOWN

The attention of most people when they are ill is focused on their bodies- on the pain, the rash, the swelling, the discomfort and they then place their bodies in the care of someone who has specialization in the subject i.e. the doctor. This is a very wise thing to do because the body is delicate, complicated and wonderful; we do not know much about it.

But the care of the body in sickness is not all that is necessary. There are other things as well to focus our attention upon like our thoughts, moods, feelings, emotions, our state of mind. Worries, fears, low feelings, stress, depressions are the real things that lead to or are the symptoms of physical disease. This is because we are in conflict with our inner self, our lower nature and higher nature (nowadays mere physical illness are very less, rather the combination of physical and mental illnesses are found in a high number). As our mind is very sensitive and a part of us, we start seeing changes in our thoughts and emotions first followed by physical symptoms.

Allport said, "Personality is neither exclusively mental nor exclusively physical. Its organization entails the functioning of both 'mind' and 'body' in some inextricable unity."

Evidently, our thoughts govern our mind and body. Indirectly, our body obeys the mind right from eating, drinking, sleeping, enjoying, etc. The body is like a mirror, reflecting whatever thoughts are running in our mind.

So, our bodily conditions depend on our thoughts and energy flows. This later materializes into altered emotions followed by physical symptoms.

Our mind is a helipad to thousands of thoughts daily out of which 90% are the same. There are no or rare new thoughts. It's like the same thoughts leading to the same choices, the same choices leading to the same behavior pattern, the same pattern triggering the same emotions and thoughts, and hence, the same personality repeats daily.

For example – your child is out for a long time and has not returned home at the given time. You start having thoughts of anxiety and emotions, worrying about him/her. You try calling but the phone is not reachable, you start getting anxious, getting into a panic mode and then finally headache sets in. This is commonly seen in most of us. Most of the time, we are not worried about these changes but when they become repetitive without you realizing that it is shaping into a pattern and becoming a part of you, bells start ringing.

Till mid-age, you start behaving in the same pattern and make it a habit unconsciously. Now when you decide to change this pattern, you start feeling uncomfortable and tend to go back to the same comfort-habitual state of yours. Hence, you need to take charge of yourself and create new patterns. In the beginning, it might be difficult but later the new you will flow. So whichever stage, cause or type of depression; reboot, connect, join your dots and start adapting to the new patterns.

In the next chapter, we will understand midlife more deeply as I stated in the beginning 'awareness is the first step to change'. So, let's comprehend the mechanics of midlife.

CHAPTER 2

UNDERSTANDING MIDLIFE

In the development of man, the age group from 40 – 60 years is considered as middle life. It is the ending of millennial life and stepping ahead into midlife.

Of all the conditions that influence our personality development, relationships between the individual and members of one's family rank first.

The term 'Personality' is derived from the Latin word Persona, which means 'mask'. Among the Greeks, actors used a mask to hide their identity on stage. This dramatic technique was later adopted by the Romans to whom persona denoted "as one appears to others" and not as actually is.

Present-day scientific concepts of personality underline the motivational as well as the behavioral aspects of personality. They emphasize not only on how the individual appears to others but what he actually is and why is he the way he is.

The hereditary factors of personality reside in the child from the moment of conception and are therefore unchangeable. But the environment leans closely upon hereditary in the development of the individual as the environment cannot originate an ability which has not already been transmitted by hereditary.

> **"Development implies qualitative change."**
> **– Van denDaele**

It means that development not only means adding inches or improving one's ability but a complex process of integrating many structures and functions.

The human being is never static. From conception to death, change is constantly taking place physically and psychologically. Even though development is continuous, as Bower has pointed out, it is a series of waves with whole segments of development reoccurring repetitively.

Early foundations are critical – Attitudes, habits and patterns of behavior established during the early years largely determine how successfully or unsuccessfully individuals will adjust to life as they grow older.

Early patterns do tend to persist but they are not unchangeable. Change may come when a person receives help and guidance. Change can also be catalyzed when there is a strong motivation on the part of individuals themselves to drive the change.

All individuals are different and each phase of development has a characteristic behavior; hazards. They are aided by stimulation, cultural changes, social expectations, traditional beliefs, etc.

Development has a major role to play in each one's life. Based on the factors stated above, we tend to develop our individual personality. Hence, different people suffer from different ailments and therefore, there cannot be a standard prescription for all of us.

What are the characteristics of midlife?

According to Desmond, 'they slump into middle age grudgingly, sadly and with a tinge of fear'. The most important trigger for fear is the belief that mental and physical energies deteriorate with the onset of middle age. This fear influences attitudes and philosophy of life.

TRANSITIONAL PERIOD – There are important physiological changes that take place during this period. Men undergo a change in virility and women find a change in fertility. This transition requires new adjustments. There are role changes, crisis and consequent problems. The main crisis is concerning parenthood, dealing with aging parents and the crisis of the untimely death of a spouse.-

Now, let's review certain factors that can cause a damaging effect on the people of this age category.

According to Hurlock, the following are the main categories of stress in middle age:

1. Somato stress, which is due to physical evidence of aging.
2. Cultural stress, stemming from the high value placed on youth, vigor and success by the cultural group.
3. Economic stress, resulting from the financial burden of educating children and providing status symbols for all family members.
4. Psychological stress, which may due to the death

of a spouse, the departure of children from home, boredom with marriage, or a sense of lost youth and approaching death.

DANGEROUS AGE – Physical breakdown due to over-work, over worry or careless living. The incidence of mental illness rises rapidly in middle age among both men and women. It is also a peak age for suicides, especially among men.

AWKWARD AGE – The middle-age men and women are neither young nor old. Therefore, they feel awkward and harbor the desire to be as much inconspicuous as possible.

PERIOD OF ACHIEVEMENT– During this period, one notices a peak of earning. Those who are ambitious reach their maximum success and start reaping the benefits of their hard work. It is a period of authority and prestige.

PERIOD OF BOREDOM AND EMPTY NEST – As children get married and well off, loneliness creeps in. Archer says, "By the time you are 40, everyone – including you know that you can do whatever you are doing. And at that point some men get bored. Some begin looking for new territory. In most men, however, the impulse is checked by the sense that one has passed the last chance to change directions to choose goals."

There are a lot of changes that occur related to interests, vocational adjustments, family life and physical wellbeing. Any of these, if not welcomed with positivity and a smile, may later lead to feeling low and eventually take the form of depression. Therefore, accepting this phenomenon and making changes accordingly will be of great benefit.

Stress and emotions play a very important role in depression along with the changes in life. Stress such as pressure, frustration, conflict, anxiety, etc. and emotions like anger, guilt, loathing, suppressions and repressions are some of the emotions that translate into depression.

In the next chapter, let's review the medical aspect of midlife. Well, do not feel apprehensive about the term 'medical'. I have tried to dissect the scientific terms in a way that even a layman to science can understand.

CHAPTER 3

MEDICAL ASPECT OF MIDLIFE

John Madina (molecular biologist) in his book "Brain Rules" has shared about the role and impact of emotions on the human brain.

Emotions are like neon signs telling your brain –remember this.

Depression seems to be a complex illness, which has a profound social impact. It is thought to be caused by an intricate variety of genetic, biochemical, psychological and circumstantial factors.

People with depression exhibit elevated levels of cortisol, which is related to brain changes in the hippocampus, prefrontal cortex and amygdala. While the hippocampus and the prefrontal cortex (which are involved in emotion regulation, memory forming and decision-making) lose volume, the amygdala (responsible for our fear and stress response) becomes enlarged and more active. Known as the "stress hormone", those with depression exhibit greater cortisol levels at all points during the day than people without depression.

Depression is also known to reduce the levels of certain GABA neurotransmitters. This, evidently, points to an association between major depressive disorders (MDDS) and diverse types of GABAergic deficits.

According to WHO, by 2030 depression will be a leading cause of disability worldwide.

Globally more than 264 million people of all ages suffer from depression in which more women are affected than men

As stated earlier, experiences vary from person to person; no two people can have an identical experience. The underlying triggering causes also can be different as every individual has a different upbringing, family, social and cultural environment, personal and professional life.

People are unaware of the initial state as to when did it really set in, and most of the time, the signs and symptoms, though felt by the person, are so vague that they are ignored. One does not realize that when he or she acquired this suffering called depression.

An estimated 10-30% of people diagnosed with depression are treatment-resistant. According to the NICE guidelines, these are the people who have not responded to courses of 2 different antidepressants. They may also be referred to counseling or cognitive behavioral therapy (CBT). People need to weigh the benefits of antidepressants with their well-reported side-effects.

In such cases, the holistic approach with alternate therapies can step in and bridge this gap. This approach can help people who are not yet diagnosed with depression, those who are on the verge of it, and also those who are already into it.

Clinical depression may be seen in various forms. According to the DSM – IV, a medical reference commonly used by health care professionals to aid in the diagnosis, a major depressive episode consists of many of the following symptoms occurring every day –

Do you suffer from any of these?
- Depressed mood for most of the day; feeling sad or empty or tearful
- Significant loss of interest or pleasure in activities that used to be enjoyable
- Significant weight loss or weight gain, decrease or increase in appetite
- Difficulty in sleeping; insomnia or sleeping too much
- Agitation or slowing down of thoughts and reduction in physical movements
- Fatigue or loss of energy
- Feeling of self-guilt, worthlessness, aimless in life, anger towards oneself mostly self-criticism
- Poor concentration, not having clarity of mind, unable to make decisions
- Thinking about self-destruction like suicide or death
- Hopeless feeling and lack of motivation
- Loss of pleasure

Do you fall into any of these categories?
- Genetically Predisposed
- Unhealthy diet (lack of nutrients)
- Childhood abuse/trauma
- Losing a job
- Death of a loved one
- Breakup in relationship/Divorce
- Failure in exam/career
- Mental torture by family/friends
- Persistent rejection by others

If yes, please don't get overwhelmed.

To combat this, I have compiled therapies in this book, which are very easy to practice while some need expert advice. Begin with the first step of awareness and take care of yourself before any symptom starts to hiss at you. The below-mentioned therapies will take care of you and will bolster you to stay healthy. It is just like building our immune system and making it so strong that we can keep most of the infections at bay. It does not mean that we are never going to suffer from anything anytime. Change is a part of life so obviously, our physical and mental state will change from time to time. However, these tools will help you adapt to change with ease. You can remain healthy, strong and acquire a balanced state of mind. In fact, when we are balanced internally, it is very easy to tackle the external factors.

CHAPTER 4

THERAPIES

It is said that for depression, we cannot have a fixed approach of treatment which is effective for a significant number of patients. Instead of getting into such debates or arguments on whether a particular system is better or not, it will be more rewarding if we attempt to know the actual role of different therapies. We must be aware of how can these therapies help or complement each other while accomplishing the ultimate goal of healing people from depression.

Disease is a state of uneasiness, anxiety, restlessness first at the mental level and if not attended, it extends to the physical level. For example, the mental state of anxiety causes tension in the mind followed by the body causing the muscles to contract followed by indigestion and a state just opposite of health appears which we call disease.

> "When mind is not in the brain how can you treat depression?" - Grace Elizabeth Jackson

Very well said by Grace. Generally, the physical symptoms in the patients are treated with mainstream medicines, which may or may not give results, especially in severe cases. Therefore, instead of treating the physical symptoms, we can always use a holistic approach to start with. This approach can be taken even before the clinical depression symptoms are seen in the patients. I have used these therapies very successfully in individual or combined ways. At my clinic, I also implement custom-tailored programs for one-to-one sessions depending on each case as every personality is unique and the causative factors for each individual are different. I always feel that each case needs to be handled differently which I follow.

Life has been very kind to us. There are so many things in life that are given to us before we reach the red alert zone called suffering, but the point is, are we really paying attention to them or just ignoring them? When learned men said that our 'body is a temple' and we need to take care of it, how many of us took it seriously? But now the time has come when we cannot ignore these teachings and instead put them to use.

I am going to accord you with a spread of therapies on the table which I have been using in my clinic successfully for many years. These are tried and tested tools that I have applied to patients of all categories. Later, in the end, I have penned a daily regime that can be followed, thereby, taking care of your mental and physical health and boosting your immunity too.

In order to treat genetically-predisposed depression, it is advised that you rely on the prescribed anti-depressants as the first line of defense and can complement with holistic therapies as well.

There are natural ways to keep yourself healthy and happy. It is just a matter of tapping in the Universe where these natural ingredients are available in abundance. If you practice the natural therapies given below, you will gain bountiful of mental and physical robustness as our body is made up of the same 5 elements which are found in the Universe. These natural therapies are very simple and doable; however, the fact is we are still not utilizing them.

THE PHYSICAL SPA

DETOX

To start with, we should know how to keep our body clean physically and energetically. And one of the ways is to detox it. One of my patients who was into a low phase of life, suffering from water brash most of the time, was unable to get rid of this. I recommended her to start taking a saltwater bath and drink the combination of salt and lemon water daily. After 10 -15 days, she was far better. The symptoms had almost disappeared. Therefore, sometimes simple procedures are very handy, provided you do them religiously.

A simple saltwater bath daily can cleanse you externally and energetically. All you need to do is apply salt to your body or add it to the bathing water.

Drinking a combination of water, lemon and Himalayan sea salt is a perfect combination and simplest way to maintain adequate levels of hydration (which can be one of the commonest factors seen in depression).

> "You can trace every sickness, every disease, every ailment to a mineral deficiency."
> - Dr. Linus Pauling, Nobel Prize Winner (twice)

Himalayan sea salt is mined by hand directly from the ancient sea salt deposits. It is less refined and therefore has naturally high mineral content. It is known for possessing 84 trace minerals, making it very healthy and nourishing. It is rich in calcium, magnesium, iron, chloride, potassium and sodium.

Research shows that sea salt helps reduce cortisol and adrenaline, 2 stress hormones by preventing dehydration.

When all 3 ingredients (water, lemon and sea salt) are combined, it becomes a healthy tonic for our body.

Some benefits are enumerated below:
- helps in hydration of the body
- prevents muscle cramps
- gives better sleep
- boosts energy levels which are very low and maintains the pH balance
- lemon helps as an antioxidant and anti-inflammatory thereby boosting immunity and detoxification
- helps maintain hormonal levels thereby adrenal, thyroid and sexual health
- helps in weight loss and many more

Salt is a natural antidepressant.

Research conducted at the University of Iowa found that salt is a natural mood-elevating substance and too little salt can lead to mild depression. The study found that too much salt leads to increase BP, heart disease and other problems.

NOTE - *If suffering from any underlying disease, please consult your doctor.*

MH

AIR BATH

Nowadays because of our sedentary lifestyle and AC environment, we are not breathing fresh air which is unhealthy for our body.

Air is of prime importance for life. One may live without food and sometimes even without water but it is impossible to survive without air even for a minute. Oxygen is essential for the various cells of the body. We obtain this oxygen from the air, therefore it is important to do deep-breathing.

The main source of oxygen on earth is vegetation such as trees, shrubs, plants, etc.

All this makes obvious that we should take barefoot walks in open spaces covered with lots of greenery such as gardens so that a lot of fresh air is inhaled along with ground-prana absorbed by the body through our soles.

Due to depression and being sedentary, the person does not feel like doing anything and stay indoors, listless and breathing shallow. It is therefore recommended to go out in the open, in the green lushes to breathe fresh air. Especially the cool breeze of early mornings, being fresh and pure and rich in oxygen, purifies the blood and the body. It also fills the mind with cheer and joy. The effects of fresh air on the body, mind and health are universally recognized.

SUN BATH

Sunlight is of prime importance for our perfect health. Being born in a tropical country, we fail to realize its importance as we get sunlight in abundance. It is often seen that in western countries where the sunlight is less, staying indoors for long periods without sunlight results in depression. So, it can be said that the sun is our life force. Our life on earth is governed by the sun. You might have observed that in the rainy or cloudy season, you tend to feel low or depressed due to insufficient sunlight or solar prana. Hence, it is difficult to imagine life without the sun on earth.

The sun showers 3 types of rays:
- ***Rays of visible (white) light*** - The white light of the sun is made up of light of 7 colors as seen in the rainbow. Each color has a specific effect on the body.
- ***Infra-red rays*** – These rays impart heat. The warmth of these rays is amazing in the winter as they relax and soothe the muscles, reduce pain and swelling if any.
- ***Ultra-violet rays*** – These rays are of special importance. Vitamin D is produced in the body by the action of ultra-violet rays falling on the skin. Sunlight is the best source of vitamin D as we all know. Dr. Hess of Columbia University has concluded on the basis of his studies that the incidence of rickets in winter increases in New York due to the insufficiency of solar radiation. Sunlight improves health and augments the resistive powers of the body.

Therefore, sunbathing is very important especially for depressive people who usually stay or rather wish to stay indoors.

The mild sunlight of the morning or the evening has a therapeutic effect on the body.

One should begin by exposing the body to sunlight for 5-10 minutes, 5 minutes on anterior and 5 minutes on posterior.

Any feeling of giddiness, fatigue or discomfort experienced is an indication of excessive exposure to the sun.

After sun-bath, a cold-water bath should be taken or the body should be wiped with a piece of cloth wrung out in cold water.

NOTE - It is advisable to avoid exposing the body to the intense midday sunlight.

CLAY/MUD THERAPY

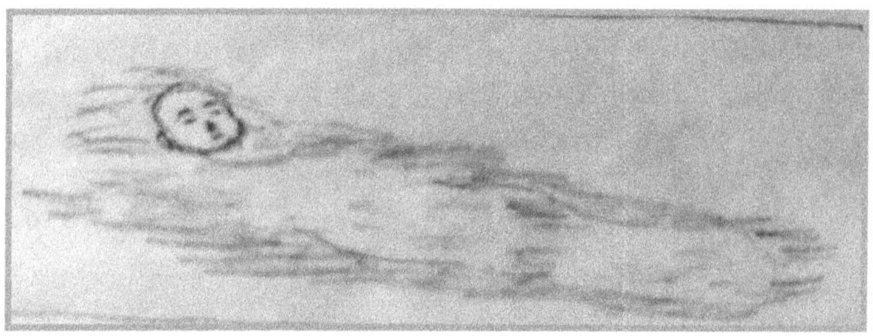

The importance of clay/mud as an external therapy or a healing agent is very similar to that of hydrotherapy.

Clay is generally used as a paste, applied directly as a pack or just like a poultice. Usually, clay is applied to the abdomen or other parts of the body which shows symptoms of the disease. If necessary, it can be applied to the whole body or a mud-bath can be taken, in which the entire body with the exception of the head is buried in the clay/mud of suitable consistency.

Lots of benefits can be derived from this therapy like:

- Cooling effect to the body
- Absorption of toxins from the body
- Reduction of swelling in the body
- Relief from pain

Relaxation is achieved as the pack reduces the tension of the muscles and soothes overstimulated nerves thereby helping to overcome depression.

All the above symptoms are seen in lots of patients with chronic stress leading to depression. I have seen a number of my patients deriving benefits from this therapy.

I generally recommend my patients that whenever they go for a vacation to the beach, always swim or take a dip in the water, then bury yourself in the sand/mud for some time and experience the magic.

In case you want to use it at home, you can apply it to your uncovered body. Make a paste of the clay/mud by adding water to it. Then spread it over to a thickness of about an inch (2.5cms.).

NOTE - Do not use any regular mud as it might not be clean or might contain harmful germs, chemicals or materials.

MASSAGE THERAPY

Massage is another therapy recommended in depression and it occupies an important place in naturopathy. Massage has been used therapeutically for thousands of years in India, China, Greece, Rome, Egypt, etc.

It is very beneficial for the skin, muscles, blood circulation, nerves and all systems of the body.

It gives a soothing and relaxing effect to the tense, sore muscles and dull mind.

The circulation of the blood in the part being massaged gets speeded up. The part is supplied with more nutrients and its healing powers are augmented.

Slow and gentle massage with light pressure relieves the tension of the nerves and soothes them. Vigorous massage stimulates lax nerves and increases their efficacy.

Massage gives you a very invigorating effect on the mind and body.

The frequency is recommended as once or twice in a month, depending on the level of stress or depression.

SUN GAZING

Sun is the bestower of life-giving light. Down the ages, ancient cultures have worshipped the Sun by building temples, shrines and monuments to pay tribute to the omnipotent 'giver of life' Sun. Also called "Lord Savitur", Sun is the powerhouse of energy called solar energy.

Sungazing simply means, gazing at the sun and manipulating photons.

Eyes are connected to the brain via the optic nerve. So, when we look into the sun, the photons and light from the sun get absorbed by our brain and stimulates our biophotons.

When sunlight hits our eyes, the optic nerve sends electric impulses to the pineal gland in turn regulating our hormonal balance.

Sunlight also has the ability to decalcify the pineal gland (seat of the soul) which has another set of life-changing benefits as it is said, "eyes are the windows of your soul". It has been found that sungazing increases the size of the pineal gland. It has been observed that as we age our pineal gland starts shrinking. But the brain scans of Hira Ratan Manak were researched by NASA and they found that his lifestyle had given him an unusually high level of endurance and perfect health. Sungazing has shown signs of the enlarged pineal gland (Edmond 1995).

It also increases the serotonin and melatonin levels. Serotonin is a happy feel-good hormone while melatonin helps you sleep well thereby helping in many cases of depression.

TIME – The best time to practice as a beginner is during the first hour of daylight and the last hour of daylight. During these periods of the day, the UV Index is 0 (very low). Since the rays are not powerful, the eyes have a chance to absorb the light from the sun.

PROCEDURE – During this practice, awareness is very important as you have to listen to your body signals. Cut all the distractions and focus on how you feel. If you feel or body feels, you do not want to continue then stop because the sunlight sending impulses to the pineal gland through optic nerve might start stimulating intuition, hence listen to your signals.

You can start with standing barefoot on the natural ground. Take deep breaths, focus your gaze on the sun for 10 sec. Relax and let go of all of the stress, tensions and worries. Blink whenever needed. Then cover your eyes with the palm of your hands. Watch the sun-afterglow fade away. It is important to move slowly to allow your eyes to adjust to the sun's light. Start looking above or below the sun (at the lower or upper ring). Once you get used to it, then you can shift to the center. You need to do the proper way. Once the sun's energy has been absorbed in this fashion, the person should walk barefoot for a period of time so that excess energy is given back to the earth, in other words, it is also called grounding.

There is scientific evidence linking walking barefoot with spiritual awakening and changes in thought processes.

A study by Dr. Turner and Dr.Mainster from the University of Kansas School of Medicine published in the British Journal of Molecule 2008 states human eyes contains photosensitive cells in the retina. These cells are directly connected to the pituitary gland and these photoreceptors play a role in physiology and health.

NOTE – Staring at the sun without proper training can/will damage your eyes.

EXERCISES

Exercises along with a good healthy diet play a very important role in maintaining mental and physical health. Our ancestors were healthier and stronger mentally and physically because they led a much more strenuous life than us.

There are different kinds of exercises that you can do.
- Exercises involving rapid movements of the body like brisk walking, jogging, running, swimming, dancing, cycling, or going to the gym, etc.

Yogasanas

You have multiple choices but I personally recommend yoga after observing the remarkable benefit in our group sessions. So, let me share a few, yet invaluable, yoga asanas with you. After reading about the benefits, you might start loving yoga and start practicing immediately.

Studies have indicated reduced levels of cortisol in those who practice yoga.

Yogasana and pranayama are the key part of yoga that induce relaxation in the body. Mindful meditation (another aspect of yoga) is also associated with lowering cortisol as well as a reduction in the size of the amygdala.

One study showed low cortisol levels, another study showed great improvement in mood than a metabolically matched walking exercise along with an acute increase in thalamic GABA levels.

Another promising study showed a reduction in suicidal thoughts.

> **"If your Autonomic Nervous System is balanced out, then the rest of the brain works better."**
> **- Dr. Chris Streeter, associate professor of Psychiatry and Neurology at**
> **Boston University of Medicine**
>
> **"Yoga allows you to find an inner peace that is not ruffled and veiled by the endless stresses and struggles of life."**
> **- BKS Iyenger**

POSES

BALASANA

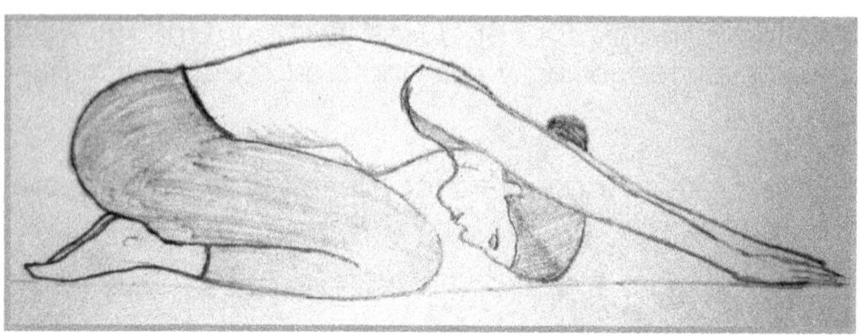

It helps calm your brain, body by stretching the lower back and spine and relieve stress and anxiety. It gives you peace of mind, helping you to deal with depression in a better way.

SETU BHANDHASANA

It strengthens the back muscles, helps you relax and works wonders for stress, anxiety and depression.

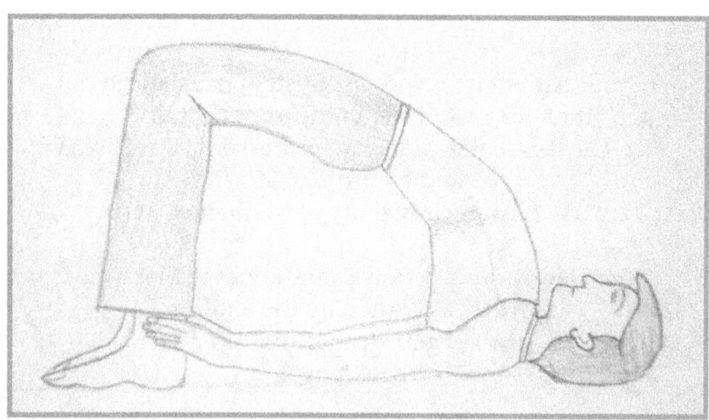

USTRASANA

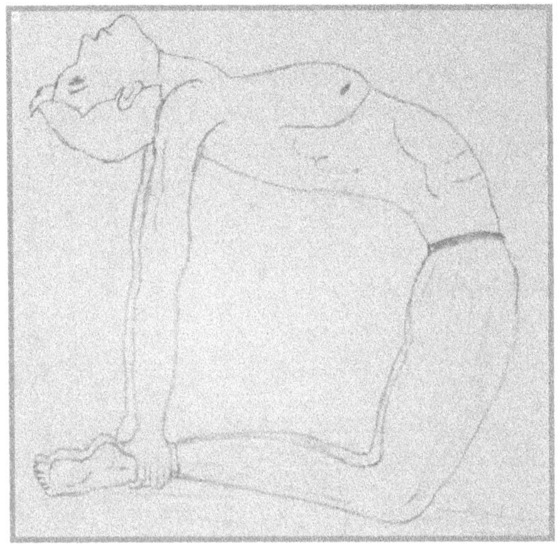

It improves the function of the nervous system, helps in calming and reducing anxiety.

MATYSASANA

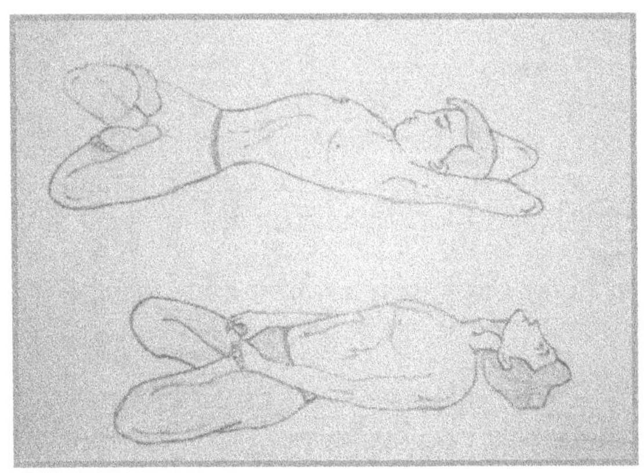

The spine becomes more supple and flexible. The respiratory system becomes more efficient. It gives a feeling of relaxation to the mind.

In case you are not able to do the 2 types of exercises (Yogasana and Pranayama), there is one yogic exercise which combines the benefits of both these type of exercises to some extent. And that is Sooryanamaskar.

SOORYANAMASKAR

The exercise should be performed preferably in the fresh open air, in the mild sunlight of early morning, deriving the benefits of the sunbathing i.e. the energy of the sun.

The total number of soorya namaskars and the speed of performing them should be increased slowly.

Optional – Recitation of mantras optimizes your vibrations, hence you can recite the Gayatri mantra before starting with the soorya namaskars.

Om Bhuur- BhuvahSvah

Tat-Savitur-Varennyam

BhargoDevasyaDhimahi

DhiyoYo Nah Prachodayaat

You can also recite the different names of the sun followed by each soorya namaskar posture.

OM MITRAY NAMAH
OM RAVAYE NAMAH
OM SURYAYE NAMAH
OM BHANAVE NAMAH
OM KHAGAYE NAMAH
OM PUSHNE NAMAH
OM HIRANYAGARBHAYE NAMAH
OM MARICHAYE NAMAH
OM ADITYAYE NAMAH
OM SAVITRE NAMAH
OM ARKAYA NAMAH
OM BHASKARAYE NAMAH

SHAVASANA

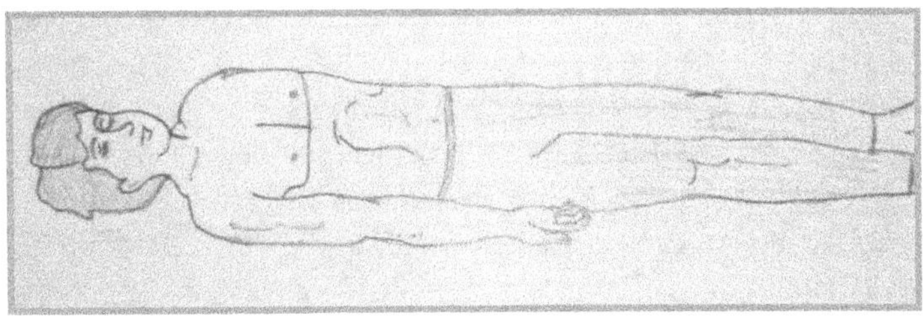

This asana is also called as the MRUTASANA. This asana can be done at the end. It relaxes the muscles and the blood vessels. Though it appears simple, it is one of the most difficult to master. This asana relaxes the mind and the body in the shortest possible way.

Benefits

The posture and the meditation are combined in shavasana, helping to soothe the body and alleviate the energy.

Shavasana helps relax all parts of the body including all muscles and nerves.

Shavasana helps the mind to recuperate in depression by feeling invigorating and refreshing.

Shavasana is an attempt to dissociate the mind from the body.

Shavasana is universally acknowledged to be the ideal for relieving the psychological ailments and tensions in today's life.

The asana consists of 3 stages –

FIRST STAGE –
Lie in the supine position (face up) on the floor without a cushion. Close your eyes. Keep the arms and legs relaxed in convenient positions. Now relax the muscles of the body, making a conscious attempt to relax each and every part of the body. Begin with the muscles of the legs. Relax and loosen them as much as you can. Then successively relax the muscles of the thighs, lower torso, upper torso, arms, neck and face, trying to make the body feel totally lifeless i.e. completely relaxed.

SECOND STAGE –
After relaxing all the muscles, turn your attention to breathing. Inhale extremely slowly and also release the breath very slowly. Continue this for some time.

THIRD STAGE –
This is the most important stage but is slightly difficult and requires practice.

The aim is to slowly and steadily sedate the mind to the ultimate level of complete cessation of thoughts. However, the desired benefit can be attained if the mind can be induced to hold on to some positive affirmation or concentrate on the breath or point in between the eyebrows (also known as the Third Eye Chakra). Initially, the mind will wander but perseverance can help calm down the mind with positivity, peace and contentment.

Duration – In the beginning, try doing it for 10 – 15 minutes daily. Later, you can decide on your own.

The Yog-Darshana Philosophy

Yog-darshana is one of the six darshanas, or ways of viewing the world, according to Hindu philosophy. The other five darshanas of Hindu philosophy are: *samkhya, nyaya, vaisheshika, mimamsa* and *vedanta*. According to yoga-darshana, the Universe is the consequence of the interaction of nature (*prakriti*) and the self (*purusha*). The ambition of yoga is to cease turbulence of the mind so the self can be liberated. These mental blockages barricade liberation. To help appease the mind, yoga-darshana requires both moral and practical steps known as the Eight Limbs of Yoga. They include:
- *Yama* – integrity, ethics

- *Niyama* – self-discipline and spiritual observance
- *Asana* – posture or pose
- *Pranayama* – breath control exercises
- *Pratyahara* – withdrawal from the external world and detachment from the senses
- *Dharana* – concentration
- *Dhyana* – meditation, contemplation
- *Samadhi* – the state of being one with the Divine; ecstasy

PRAYANAMAS

When you sit in one convenient asana and regulate the act of respiration, it is called pranayama.

By practicing this, you not only inhale and exhale the air but also the prana which is available in abundance in the cosmos. This helps you keep your body and mind healthy.

As the fire cleanses the dross elements contained in the gold when heated, in the same manner, PRANAYAMA CLEARS THE BODY AND THE MIND.

Hath Yoga Pradpikais a classic fifteenth-century Sanskrit manual on haṭha yoga, written by Svātmārāma.*Pradipika* means "light" or "to illuminate", Hatha Yoga is the science of yoga, which purifies the physical body.

According to this scripture, prana and mind are closely related to each other. By controlling the breath, the mind automatically concentrates.

Pranayama has the capacity of freeing the mind from ignorance, painful and unpleasant experiences hence it is advisable to practice pranayama regularly. So, let me share some pranayama asanas.

DEEP ABDOMINAL BREATHING

Concentrate on your stomach while taking deep breaths. In the beginning, you can also keep one palm on the abdomen to exactly know the movement of the abdomen while you inhale and exhale. Start inhaling deeply and observe the abdomen expanding outwards and when you exhale observe the abdomen going inwards, trying to make a scaphoid abdomen. This is the right way to breathe. You can start with 5 counts first and then as you get comfortable, you can increase the counts.

Once you become proficient in your abdominal breathing pattern, you can slowly start the practice of pranayama.

PRANAYAM MAKES YOUR MIND CALM AND KEEPS YOU HAPPY!

BHASTRIKA PRANAYAMA

Sit in a comfortable asana. Breathe in through both the nostrils forcefully, till the lungs are full and diaphragm stretched. Then breathe out forcefully, but ensure that the abdominal cavity does not blow up due to the air breathed in. Depending on the capacity and the health of an individual, this pranayama can be done in 3 variable speeds viz slow, moderate and high speed. Individuals with weak lungs and heart should do this at a slow speed. A normal physically healthy individual can start with slow speed and then gradually increase to moderate and high. It should be done for 5 – 10 minutes.

While doing the pranayama, focus on your mind as if all the divine powers, purity, peace and joy and all that is good in the Universe around you are entering inside you and you are filled with lots of positivity. This pranayama will benefit you multifold.

KAPALA- BHATI PRANAYAMA

Kapala means forehead and Bhati means light. It means this exercise makes your forehead luminous. This pranayama is slightly different than the bhastrika. In bhastrika, you inhale and exhale with the same amount of force but in kapala-bhati, more attention is to be given to the forceful exhalation whereas inhalation is done with normal force. In doing so, the abdominal area also makes inward and outward movements.

This pranayama can be done for five minutes. In short, inhaling is normal and the exhalation is forceful.

While doing this pranayama visualize that while exhaling you are throwing all the diseases out of the body. Individuals with negative emotions like anger, irritability, anxiety, stress, depression should feel that all these negative feelings are being driven out of the body along with the exhaled air.

Hence, to be precise, it is a shudhi kriya (detoxifying exercise), wherein you try to clean up your internal dirt be it physical or emotional out of the body thereby making it healthy.

ANULOM-VILOM

This is done by closing the nostrils alternately. Close the right nostril with the thumb of the right hand, and likewise close the left nostril with the middle and ring fingers, keeping the palm just above the nose.

This pranayama helps in purification of the nadis and thus maintaining the balance.

Now, let me share the step-by-step process. Close your right nostril with the thumb of the right hand. Inhale slowly through the left nostril till the lungs are filled. Then close the left nostril with the middle and the ring fingers. Open the right nostril and exhale through it. Repeat the exercise slowly in the beginning and with practice, you can increase the speed and force of inhalation and exhalation. With proper practice, this pranayama can be done for 5 to 10 minutes.

While performing this pranayama, there is a flow of divine energy coming down, giving you peace, calmness and balance.

BHRAMARI

Breathe in till your lungs are full. Close your ears with both the thumbs and eyes with the middle fingers on the respective sides with little pressure. Press the forehead lightly with both the index fingers. Close both the eyes. Then press the eyes and nose bridge from the sides with the remaining fingers. Concentrate your mind at the midpoint of the eyebrows. Close your mouth. Begin exhaling slowly, making a humming sound of a bee. Repeat the exercise according to your capacity or for 11 to 12 times.

With this practice of pranayama, the mind becomes steady and releases the mental tension, stress and agitation.

TRATAK – It is an exercise in which the sight is fixed on a particular object.

Sit in the normal sukhasana position. Place a burning candle or a picture of a black dot at a distance of one and a half or 2 feet away from the face. Look at that object without straining the eyes. Hold back the winking of the eyes. When the eyes are tired or they shed water, close them and imagine the picture of that object. Open your eyes again after some time and practice tratak again. Do this exercise 4-5 times.

BENEFITS – Tratak strengthens the eyes and make them brighter. Indirectly, it has a beneficial effect on the brain and the mind thereby helping in depression.

NOTE - If tratak is not performed properly, the eyes may be damaged. Therefore, it is necessary to practice this exercise under the guidance of an expert.

NUTRITIONAL HEALTHY DIET

A healthy diet is very important for patients of depression. It is seen that depressive patients do not get the necessary amounts of carbohydrates, proteins, essential fatty acids, vitamins and minerals required for our body.

The macrobiotic diet promotes the growth of good bacteria in our body and removes foods that harm the survival of good bacteria in our body. The foods that promote the growth of good bacteria include a lot of pre-biotic and pro-biotic foods in our diet like yogurt, sauerkraut, fruits and vegetables and a lot of other organic foods. The foods that can be removed/changed from the diet may include the following:

- Removing refined sugar, honey and other sugar substitutes; replacing them with fruits and organic coconut sugar (in very limited quantities)
- Removing dairy products except for yogurt and ghee. Replacing dairy-based milk with home-made almond milk
- Removing gluten-based wheat and its derivatives like maida(flour) and others and replacing them with other flours like jowar (sorghum), ragi, bajra (millet), etc.
- Replacing refined vegetable oils in cooking with cold-pressed oils
- Replacing refined salt with pink/rock salt (Himalayan salt)
- Replacing refined white rice with brown or red rice/poha
- Eliminating all non-veg foods including eggs
- Eliminating all processed foods and junk foods and sugary drinks
- Stoppage of all restaurant and outside foods

- Increasing the intake of raw vegetables (in the form of salads and juices) and fruits. The focus should be on eating cooked meals 3 times a day. Apart from that eat 2 servings of raw vegetables and fruits during the day. Daily lunch should include salad made of carrots, beetroots, cucumber, etc. Evening snack can include a banana and 1-2 other seasonal fruits.
- Increasing the intake of all types of millets like foxtail, little, proso, barnyard millet, finger millets, etc. You can add Turmeric, black pepper, ginger and garlic paste, powdered cloves, flaxseeds, sesame seeds, aloe vera juice, triphala juice to the vegetable juice. You can take any 3-4 vegetables (spinach, beetroot, carrots, tomatoes, cucumber, celery) juice and add the juice to the spices concoction in the glasses. You can also take lemon juice and celery juice in the morning and vegetable juice in the afternoon daily to enhance the immunity.
- Post dinner you can have a serving of seasonal fruit. Jowar or millet laddus made with organic coconut sugar and dry fruits can be taken as desserts.

ESSENTIAL OILS

Essential oils and its extracts have been used externally, internally and by olfaction, for centuries as a treatment for anxiety and depression.

Essential oils have a high concentration of volatile oils, which impart a distinctive and pleasing fragrance. The relaxing experience of the fragrance leads to its deliberate, therapeutic use in aromatherapy to relieve mild anxiety. It is also used for mood imbalances such as anxiety, insomnia and gastrointestinal distress, including a nervous stomach.

Lavender oil can be sprayed in your bedroom for a peaceful sleep. It can be used as a burner/diffuser to relieve stress and improper moods and as an olfactory mode.

Rose oil can be used in fear, stress. One can apply it to the heart area or use it as an olfactory mode.

Lemon, Peppermint and Clove oil can be used to activate the vagus nerve and balance the emotions.

ACUPRESSURE

All the acupressure points, when practiced regularly along with other therapies, help in the miraculous healing of depression.

PROCEDURE – Apply firm pressure on the given points for 2-3 minutes and then release it or you can slightly massage at certain points.

Sea of Tranquility (CV17)

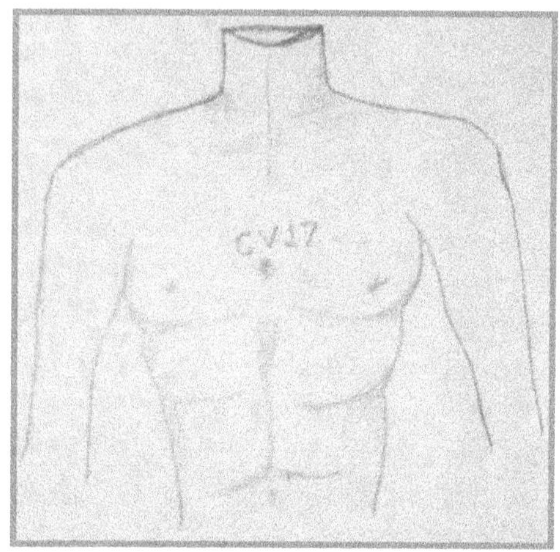

Third-eye point

Lungs 1 Point (LU1)

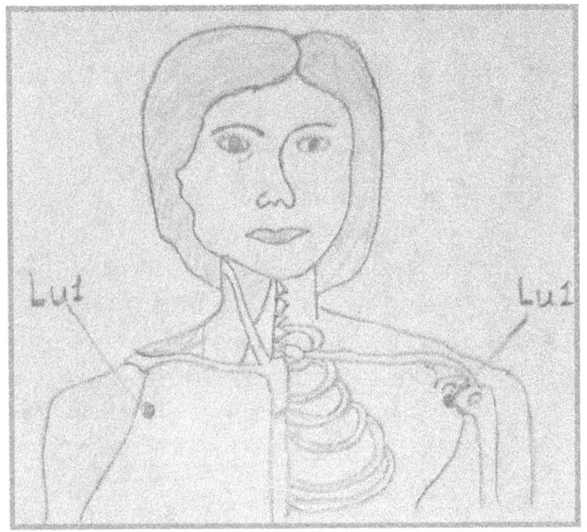

One Hundred Meeting Point (GV20)

EMOTIONAL FREEDOM TECHNIQUE – EFT

It is a technique in which various alternative therapies are put together to benefit people from emotional problems like stress, anxiety and depression.

It follows the similar principle of acupressure of releasing the blocked energies from the clogged meridians. By tapping the meridians, signals are sent to the amygdala thereby rewiring the connections and releasing unwanted emotional energies.

The individual taps on meridian endpoints of the body such as the top of the head, eyebrows, under eyes, side of eyes, chin, collar bone, 3 inches under the arms and top of the head reciting phrases of the emotion.

Some practitioners incorporate eye movements or inhaling and exhaling during the use of the technique.

It can also be done with the recitation of positive affirmations.

MUDRAS

Mudras are hand gestures that help the free flow of energy by channelizing or directing energy to the body. Mudras have been used for thousands of years for providing relief in various problems. For depression or the symptoms before depression, practice these 2 mudras which are very effective:

PROCEDURE – use the fingers to make the mudra which you want to practice and slightly press the tips of the fingers where they join. This allows the release of blockages of the meridians related to the mudra.

CHIN MUDRA/DYAN MUDRA – helps in gaining and maintaining alertness of the mind, clarity. Also, helps in overall mood elevation.

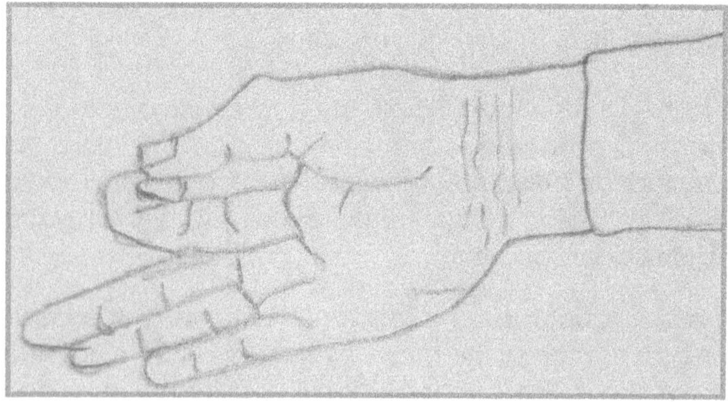

\# KALESVARA MUDRA – relaxes agitation, nervousness and anxiety of the mind thereby bringing calmness and relaxation to the mind.

THE MENTAL SPA

Everything first happens in the mind and then on the physical plane. Therefore, it is very important to reprogram your identity if you want to see results. Now that we have started with our physical spa, we need to follow it with a mental spa to reap the benefits. So, here are the techniques you may practice for your mental spa.

AFFIRMATIONS

It is the act where we try to confirm something to believe in it. Affirmation is a statement intended to provide encouragement, emotional support, or motivation, especially when used for the purpose of autosuggestion.

Nowadays, positive affirmations are becoming very popular as there is a genuine theory and a fair amount of neuroscience behind this practice.

It is a science, not magic, so would you like to know more about it?

One of the key psychological theories behind positive affirmations is self-affirmation theory (Stele 1988). Yes, there are studies based on the idea that we can maintain our sense of self-integrity by telling ourselves in positive ways.

Maintaining self-integrity is very important in life. There is MRI evidence suggesting that certain neural pathways are amplified when people practice self-affirmation task (Cascio et al, 2016). To be specific, the ventromedial prefrontal cortex involved in positive valuation and self-related information processing becomes more active when we consider our personal values (*Falk et al., 2015; Cascio et al., 2016*).

Affirmation is an oral or a written statement, which can be repeated several times in a day.

I recommend each and every patient of mine with customized affirmations according to their emotional state and compliment them with other therapies.

You can write down the affirmations and recite them daily for any number of times or you can record them in your voice and listen to them whenever possible during the day.

Some daily affirmations that you can practice:
- I believe in myself!
- I choose to be happy with myself!
- These are just the present moments and they do not define me who I am!

- I release all the negative feelings and thoughts about myself!
- I love myself!
- I am getting better and better daily!
- I do not need to rely on other's acceptance!
- I do not rely on other's judgments!
- I am confident and have the resilience to handle my life!
- I am getting confident day by day!

According to Louise Hay, affirmations are great to practice, by looking at oneself in the mirror and reciting them in the morning can be very powerful. It's the best time as it can decide how your whole day can go.

GRATITUDE

It is the quality of being thankful, readiness to show appreciation for and to return kindness.

It's important to be grateful in life. You can express gratitude starting from small things like feeling gratitude as soon as you open your eyes in the morning, knowing that you are alive. There are many people who do not wake up to see the new day.

Sometimes while looking at the larger things in life, we fail to see so many small good things which life has given us like a healthy body, home, parents, food, clothes, education and much more. If we really introspect or sit down to write, the list is endless. We might finish a

notebook penning down the things (no pun intended). We are so much lost in big things that we are unable to appreciate the small things that we are blessed with. Try looking around you, especially at the people below you; you might have understood what I am trying to say here.

There might be things you are deprived of, there might be some or many depressing moments in life. However, at the same time, I would suggest you not to let the wick of your faith fade away.

> **"In every situation (no matter what the circumstances) be thankful and continually give thanks to God for this is the will of God for you in Christ Jesus"**
> **– Thessalonians**

BENEFITS OF BEING GRATEFUL/THANKFUL

It not only helps in sprucing up your mind but your body too:
- Immune system becomes stronger
- Reduces stress
- Brings more joy, happiness and optimism.
- Makes you more resilient
- Lowers high blood pressure
- Makes you feel less lonely and isolated

In our childhood, we were taught to be thankful to God for whatever he has given us. Our young ears were often instructed, "As soon as you wake up in the morning and put your feet on the ground, pray and be thankful to the Mother Earth, be grateful and pray before you eat your meal," and so on. Our strong culture has taught many things to mankind but in this rat race, we have lost a great treasure which we are unaware of.

So, let us try to revive this virtue –
- Focus your attention on all the processes happening outside, starting from getting up in the morning until going to bed.
- Thank God for the material possessions that you have.
- Keep a Gratitude Journal. Keep a record of whatever you feel grateful for in the Journal on a regular basis.

It has been seen that people who maintain the Gratitude Journal report fewer health problems.

Be aware of the positive things in life and do not just concentrate on the negative things.

No one is 100% happy and nobody can possess everything in life, so be thankful for whatever you have in life and move on.

IKIGAI

Wikipedia defines Ikigai as a Japanese concept that means "a reason for being". The word refers to having a direction or purpose in life, which makes one's life worthwhile. This is the purpose towards which an individual takes spontaneous and willing actions, giving him/her satisfaction and a sense of meaning to life.

The term Ikigai compounds 2 Japanese words "ki" meaning life, alive and "kai" meaning effect, result, fruit, etc.

Many a time we lack focus, purpose in our lives, we start feeling hopeless and aimless. We start questioning ourselves about our existence and are unable to find answers. This is the time when we find ourselves heading to a dark tunnel.

Ikigai depicts the idea that everyone has their own reason for being and its revealed at the intersection of the 4 pillars; your passion, mission, vocation and profession.

You can have a checklist of this. You can start looking at things differently, asking questions to yourself, changing your perspectives in these 4 areas of your life. Once you get a deeper understanding of yourself, you will find your answers. This is one way to come out of depression. For the ones who are left-brain-users, on a quest to find answers to their 'WHY', and are willing to take action; this can be great therapy for them.

BACH FLOWER REMEDIES

In the healing system through flower remedies discovered by Dr. Edward Bach, the medicine is selected individually. That is, the patient's FEELINGS are considered for the selection of remedies.

These remedies could be used in conjunction with any other form of treatment and would not clash or interfere. Though these cannot be strictly classified as 'medicine' we must bear in mind the fact that these are 'regulators' of the human mind and can be complemented with other therapies for depression.

MUSTARD – Black depression of unknown cause

PINE – Self-blame, self-reproach, feeling of guilt, despondency

GENTIAN – Depression, sadness, discouragement, uncertainty

WILLOW – Blaming others, resentment, bitterness

SCLERANTHUS –Indecision or hesitation from uncertainty

HONEYSUCKLE – Dwelling too many mistakes and memories from the past

LARCH – Lack of confidence, expectation of failure, despondency

OLIVE – Extreme exhaustion, complete tiredness of mind and body

HORNBEAM– Mental and physical tiredness and weariness

WHITE CHESTNUT- Unwanted persistent thoughts. Mental arguments and conversations

Bach flower remedies work on emotional levels, helping to balance them.

HOMOEOPATHY

Homeopathy was discovered by Dr. Hahnemann in the late 18 century. It is a therapeutic system of medicine based on the principle of 'Similia Similibus Curentur' or 'Likes Cure Likes'. It is a method of curing the patient by medicines that possess the power of producing similar symptoms in a healthy human being. Homeopathy stimulates the natural disease which can be cured in the diseased person. The patient is treated not only through a holistic approach but also considers the individualistic characteristics of the person.

Homeopathy has gained a lot of importance in recent years due to various reasons. More people are opting for homeopathy due to its amazing results. Homeopathy deals with the mind first followed by physical symptoms, hence distinctly applicable in depression, though all kinds of diseases can be treated by homeopathy. Being a homeopath myself, I have treated hundreds of cases of depression.

NOTE – Please avoid self-prescription and see a proficient homeopathy doctor for the best results.

COUNSELING

We are losing the human connection as we are going more hi-tech.

Counseling is a very important aspect of depression. Individual counseling is considered the heart of counseling where one-to-one interaction is done with the patient and the patient can seek advice and solutions to his problems or can just let out called catharsis. This is very therapeutic. People suffering from depression can also seek group counseling as one can gain a lot of insight and understanding his own problems through listening to others in the group and discussing their difficulties. Your ideas and values might be more acceptable in a group, helping you immensely.

Social engagement is very important.

Letting it out or discussing it with likeminded people may help you come out of the depression faster than anything else.

In this, you can also help resolve your relationship with others by understanding their part and forgiving them by letting go of the grudges that you have been carrying for years. We need to understand that unless you release these burdens, you cannot be free of them. Gradually start forgiving people who have hurt you for you to have and maintain inner peace.

Daily before sleeping, you can make a protocol of saying a prayer of forgiveness.I can vouch that you will definitely see the results. I make it a point to all my patients to practice forgiveness every day. I often conduct a 40-day forgiveness program which helps people tremendously to come out of their pitiful situations.

It is very important to reprogram your identity if you want to see the results.

PRANIC HEALING

A newly married lady visited me one day. She looked very much perturbed when she entered my clinic.

After analyzing her case and seeing the psychodynamics, I found that she had suppressed her emotions right from her childhood (feeling abandoned) till that given day. She suffered all by herself and never shared her feelings with anyone. Most of the time I have seen people ignoring their feelings, emotions and suffering silently until it takes the form of some disease or symptom. The same happened with this lady as well.

After listening to her case, I started psychotherapy along with Advance Pranic healing. The beauty of this treatment is you can heal a person emotionally and physically at the same time. This is unlike mainstream medicine where you need to seek different specialists for different ailments. She was completely healed after 12 sessions. Along with counseling and some other techniques, her relationship with her husband also improved. Now she is completely alright and living a happy life.

After knowing about this kind of result and a complete change in her, you might be wondering what exactly is PranicHealing?

Pranic Healing is an ancient science and art of healing that utilizes prana or ki or life energy to heal the whole physical body. Prana is that life energy that keeps the body alive and healthy.

Master Choa Kok Sui is the founder of Pranic Healing and Modern Arhatic Yoga. He started Pranic healing in 1987 and as of today, it is being practiced in 120 countries.

Pranic Healing is both pragmatic and tangible, based on the ancient esoteric principles.

Pranic healing is a no-touch, no-drug method that utilizes the prana which is abundant in the cosmos primarily in 3 forms – the sun prana, the air prana and the ground prana.

Pranic healing, in its existing form, has been painstakingly, systematically, and scientifically developed, and taught globally. Hundreds and thousands of students have learned to do Pranic Healing and millions of patients have been healed or relieved.

Pranic healing is based on the overall structure of the human body. Man's whole body is actually composed of 2 parts; the visible physical body and the invisible energy body called the bioplasmic body. The visible physical body is the one which we see, touch and are most acquainted with. The bioplasmic body is that invisible luminous energy body which is also called the energy body or etheric body.

Pranic healing is based on 2 laws – the Law of Self-Recovery and the Law of Prana or Life-Energy. These laws are quite obvious but strangely and usually, they are the least noticed or least remembered by most people. It is through these basic laws that rapid or miraculous healing occurs.

For centuries, it has been believed that clairvoyant people actually see an aura surrounding ordinary individuals, and this aura differed from person to person in color and character, expressing the health, emotional and spiritual attributes of the subject.

Pranic Healing caters to this aura thereby, healing the person physically emotionally and spiritually as there is an intimate relationship between the energy body and the physical body. Both the energy body and physical body are so closely related that what affects the one, affects the other and vice-versa.

Due to the dedicated work by Master Choa Kok Sui, there is an increasing awareness of the effect of energy (prana) on emotional and mental issues. Stress and negative emotions stored in the body create blockages in the body's energy system. When the body's healing energy becomes blocked and cannot flow properly, then disease occurs. Hence, Pranic Psychotherapy is a very powerful tool in healing emotional and psychological ailments as the removal of emotional blocks can immensely improve the overall health of the person. This is done by using unique techniques to remove the blocks. It can be used in stress, anxiety, depression, grief, traumas, phobias, etc.

Pranic psychotherapy provides a new energetic dimension to the therapeutic process and is intended to complement, augment and enhance traditional approaches.

These techniques are simple and effective and I have seen miraculous results in my patients after applying these techniques. If accompanied by a powerful yet simple meditation called meditation on twin hearts, the benefits are mind-blowing.

Pranic Healing is very effective and practiced in all kinds of major and minor ailments e.g. from simple cold and cough to alarming cancers.

You can heal all kinds of problems like physical, emotional, mental, relationship, etc.

You can heal patients even if they have not been diagnosed.

There are no side-effects in this therapy.

The uniqueness of this healing is you can use it as a preventive measure before you get unwell or suffer from any illness (you do not need to wait until you suffer from any illness – mental or physical).

This healing involves simple techniques to stay healthy, fit and happy.

The best part is anyone can learn this healing as it is very easy to learn. It is very effective and can be used for you and your family to start with and later, you might help others too.

Pranic healing also includes aura healing as by the law of correspondence, any diseased energy in the aura if not taken care of, will eventually enter the physical body.

The Ancient Science and Art of Pranic Healing-Master Choa Kok Sui

CRYSTAL THERAPY - And all these healings can also be done with the help of different crystals to see fabulous results. Crystals have their own consciousness hence crystals can be used for healing. Crystal-healing helps in removing negative emotional energies from the aura and chakras by balancing them and making them healthy thereby healing depression, stress, trauma, etc.

MEDITATION

Meditation on Twin Hearts is a very easy meditation to learn and can be practiced by anyone. I usually recommend all my patients to do this meditation daily as it gives stress relief, inner peace and happiness. We conduct regular practice sessions for the same so that all my patients practice it.

It is also a form of service to the world because the world is harmonized to a certain degree through the blessings of the entire earth with loving-kindness.

The twin hearts refer to the heart chakra which is the center of the emotional heart and the crown chakra which is the center of the divine heart.

In the case of most people, the other chakras are quite activated. The basic chakra, sex chakra and solar plexus chakra are activated practically in all people. Their instincts for self-survival, sex-drive and their tendency to react to their lower emotions are very active. With the pervasiveness of modern education and work that requires the use of mental faculty, the Ajna(third-eye) chakra and the throat chakra are developed in a lot of people. The heart chakra and the crown chakra, however, are not developed in most people. Modern education, unfortunately, tends to over-emphasize the development of the throat chakra and Ajna chakra or the development of the concrete mind and abstract mind. The development of the heart chakra has been neglected. Because of this, you may encounter a person who is quite intelligent but very abrasive. These types of people have under-developed heart chakra. Although the person may be intelligent and 'successful' as well but his human relationships may be very poor, he may hardly have any friends and may have no family. By practicing twin heat meditation, a person becomes harmoniously balanced, meaning the major chakras are more or less balanced and developed.

The Ancient Science and Art of Pranic Healing-Master Choa Kok Sui

JOURNALING

You can make a workbook and write down the behavior or habit which you feel you want to change. Write it in detail. Keep it personal.
- What do you want to change in your life?
- Why do you want to change?
- What is the cause?
- What difference will it make in your life if you change?

You can ask many more questions to yourself. Detailing is very important. Write these questions on the left side of the page. On the right side, pen down the answers to these questions. Many a time, we do not have clarity.

Once clarity is established, it becomes very easy to seek solutions.

VISUALISATION TECHNIQUE

After writing the change you want to be or make, start visualizing it. Visualizing is very important. You do not have to actually do anything but just sit, visualize the change that you want in you, just like you watch the movie but in this visualization movie, you the hero. You can create a mental theatre of it.

Everything first happens in the mind. Your subconscious mind is not aware of what is imaginary and what is real. It just follows what is fed. Hence you can use this technique to change your habits, behavioral patterns, etc. Take one behavior at a time.

For example, you want to wake up early. Visualize that on the earlier night, you made your bed, went to the table or your mobile, adjusted the alarm to 6 am. Then you went back to your bed, curled yourself, closed your eyes and went off to sleep. Early morning, you are watching yourself in bed, the alarm is ringing, you are trying to snooze it but the alarm is still ringing. You realize that you have made a promise to yourself to get up early last night. With much regret and irritation, while massaging your half-closed eyes irritation, you get up, run to splash water on your face so that you do not sneak to your tempting bed to lie down again....

You can edit this movie for ten days. You can use all your creativity like color, drama, action, humor to make it real. Do this exercise for 21 days to see the new you.

MISCELLANEOUS THERAPIES

Laughter therapy is very important. You can do the happy Buddha posture and laugh it out. First, it will be forceful but later you will start enjoying it.

Cultivate hobbies like reading, writing, dancing, painting, drawing, etc. Pet therapy, Sound therapy, Music therapy especially oceanic music is very therapeutic.

CHAPTER 5

TESTIMONIALS

CASE - 1

I, Gopal, will share the health benefits that I, my Dad and my other family members experienced by changing our diet and adopting alternative healing therapies. Today, my Dad is 65 years old and by God's grace, he is in fine fettle and free of all medications, except for one homeopathic medication. Healthwise, he is doing well for the last 1 year or so.

Chains of events that happened during the decade: 2000 to 2010

Before that, the last 8 years of his life (2010 to 2018) were pretty bad in terms of health. Even before 2010, my Dad experienced constipation and gas problems for decades, but they did not bother him. Also, during the decade 2000 to 2010, my Dad went through some traumatic events like losses in one business as his partner who ran the business left him, closure of the 2nd business due to very little sale, not being able to buy a house and staying in a rented house for 10+ years, betrayal by a childhood friend while buying a house, not being able to get a suitable groom for his daughter for almost a decade, bad relationship and power struggle with his younger son, etc. All the above events happened one after the other or in parallel and made life stressful for my Dad.

Finally, all this led to severe anxiety problems for my Dad. Before this, my family had never seen anyone suffering from anxiety and we hence did not know what it meant.

While the treatments did not work, over months, my Dad developed his own stories of presenting symptoms of how he did not feel well. He thought he was not able to breathe properly, his stomach veins were not functioning properly, he started living in fear. Dad actually started experiencing pain and other problems. But none of the diagnostic tests could diagnose them as these things did not exist in reality and they were just the figment of my Dad's imagination. Dad's health only deteriorated over time. At night, he would get 2-4 hours of sleep at the best. He lost interest in work and everything else. Constant thoughts of ill health bothered him. Finally, he attempted suicide. This came as a big shock to the entire family as even in the wildest of the dreams we never expected him to take such a step. During the hospital stay, while my Dad was under the care of a gastroenterologist, he recommended that we take a second opinion from a psychiatrist. The psychiatrist came and based on my Dad's symptoms, she said that he was suffering from anxiety. We got a good psychiatrist, and under his care, my Dad's health and mood improved, albeit only temporarily. During our interactions with psychiatrists and homeopaths, we were told about various causes of my Dad's underlying anxiety like Irritable Bowel Syndrome – IBS (as it's a psychosomatic condition), general anxiety disorder (GAD), psychosis, trauma-induced anxiety, etc. While all these diagnoses seemed like various labels to me, the common treatment protocol included anti-depressants. I read about the experiences of scores of people on the internet on how anti-depressants gave temporary relief and then the effects taper out, but people could not get off them due to the addictive nature.

Introduction to the world of alternative therapies

With anti-depressants, I started seeing a similar pattern in my Dad also. He would feel better for a few months with one medicine. Then the effect would taper out and the psychiatrist would either increase the dosage or add an additional anti-depressant. This temporary improvement bought me some time to explore the world of alternative therapies. I started exploring alternative therapies along with continuing my Dad's psychiatry treatment for anxiety. I started exploring dietary changes, yoga, mudras, emotional freedom technique (EFT), acupressure, hypnotherapy, sun gazing, barefoot grass walking, nutritional supplements, meditation, positive affirmations, energy medicine, pranic healing, spirituality, shamanism, essential oils, Fengshui, visiting various religious places for divine intervention, doing charity, forgiving and seeking forgiveness, journaling gratitude, doing various poojas, showing my Dad's horoscope to various Pandits and every other possibility under the sun to heal my Dad. You see, how desperate I was for a solution.

Dietary changes, sun gazing, barefoot walking and EFT improved my Dad's condition a lot.

Emotional detoxification

Along with the physical detoxification of the body with dietary changes, we had to do detoxification of the mind. My Dad was carrying a lot of emotional baggage of the traumatic events that happened during the 2000-2010 decade. Also, during the anxiety years, he had developed a lot of negativity which very evidently reflected in his thoughts, words and actions. So, it was essential to relieve him from these traumas and negative mindset through emotional detoxification. Emotional Freedom Technique (EFT) played a big part in helping my Dad getting rid of the emotional baggage that he was carrying. EFT helped in neutralizing the negative effects of the traumas, negative thoughts or negative bent of mind that my Dad had developed with regards to his health, overcoming resistance to adopting the macrobiotic diet, coping with effects of stopping anti-depressants.

How is my Dad's health faring now?

By God's grace, my Dad is doing well now. We stopped all the anti-depressants for my Dad more than a year back. My Dad still experiences some anxiety once in a while, but that is manageable without any medication. The anxiety has now got to do with his mindset because he still believes that he is not fully cured. Whereas, I, my family, and others who have seen my Dad during the anxiety years, believe that my Dad is absolutely fine now. His digestion has improved, he sleeps well and goes about his daily work routine along with enjoying and playing with his grandchildren. We also continue with spirituality, practicing forgiving and seeking forgiveness, and charity to enjoy the blessings of others.

How did the crisis change me as a person?

For me, the entire experience of the last few years has changed me completely as a human being. My faith in God and spirituality has become deep-rooted. I practice charity and seek the blessings of others. I believe that my and my family's health is my own responsibility. I have now come to believe that "Food is medicine". I believe the Universe has all the answers to our questions, we just need to ask or find them. I empathize with people and try to be as humble as I can, so as to not hurt anyone. Overall, I am working towards being a better human being!

CASE - 2

I, Dr. Swati, lost my husband to cancer in 2019. Life was not easy after that, with an 8years old son by my side, though I had the support of my parents. Things, circumstances and people around me changed especially their attitude and approach towards me. Some were feeling pity for me, some sorry and some wanted to take advantage. On the other hand, some of my relatives waited for the money which I was going to get from my husband's office.

This was really the funny part as people who were never good to me, suddenly, became a paragon of virtue and caring about me and my son.

After receiving the money, if I didn't respond to their wishes, I would become a big villain in their eyes.

I had never seen people like that. I come from a family where people are important and money is kept secondary but here the situation was completely opposite.

First, the loss of my husband and then the people's approach towards me made me really depressed and low. I started thinking about why that was happening to me? What did I do that it had happened to me? I didn't do any wrong to anyone then why me? All these questions depressed me a lot and to add salt to the injury, I was unable to find the answers.

These thoughts had not come to my mind even when I got the news of my husband's cancer. During that time, I was mentally strong and prepared for the future. I had also prepared my son for what would happen in the future, but this time it was different; I lost my confidence and was very low.

I wanted to speak my mind or to someone and understand what was really wrong.

I didn't know what to do, where to go.

And when you are depressed, taking medication is only one of many treatment options.

But only medication didn't help much. I would often eat unhealthy food because it was easy, and sugary foods would boost my mood for a while, but after a few hours, my energy level and mood would plummet and I would feel really lousy. Being a doctor eating unhealthy food made me more depressed as I was putting on weight. When I realized this, I decided to eat healthy food. This was the first step towards my self-realization.

Now that I eat mostly vegetables, beans, and whole grains, I feel better and feel a lot more energetic. I don't think I could have got over my depression if I had not changed my diet regime.

I needed more than just medication and a healthy diet has been something like a holistic approach towards my problem.

A holistic approach focuses on treating your whole body and mind to help you feel better. A healthy diet, exercise, and talk therapy are a few of the holistic approaches we can use, along with medication, to trigger a speedy recovery from depression.

This is where I learned about Pranic healing and meditation. I knew my friend Dr.VAISHALLI practices Pranic Healing so I met her and that made the biggest change in my life. I started practicing Twin Heart Meditation, forgiveness sessions and lots of affirmations with her help and my life changed drastically. My self-approach changed. I started loving myself and that gave me lots of positivity which helped me bounce back by regaining my confidence.

I was able to take care of the things and my son too as I neglected him due to my problems. Now my outlook towards life has changed me completely. Things around me have become more pleasing and happy.

I Feel lucky to Have met Her and understand a new way to live life Positively and Happily. Dr. Vaishalli has played a very consequential role in what I am today.

A holistic treatment where you are treated not just physically, but mentally with the help of medication, proper diet and Most importantly, the Mental treatment with counseling and meditation.

CASE – 3

Hi, I am Minaz. I received a message from Dr.Vaishalli, asking for my testimonial on how I overcame depression. I enthusiastically replied that I would feel more than happy and proud if my story can heal or motivate someone and I thank the Almighty for that. I have now been married for 18 years. My husband is working as an insurance advisor and is at a good post and I am a businesswoman. We had started from scratch and our life was going well. Life brought many challenges, showed us many ups and downs, odds and evens, yet we stood strong and triumphed over the bad times. I have two sons. Life was all set, but on 20th June 2018 a challenge appeared in our life, my father passed away all of a sudden and from there my life changed. On Friday my father wanted to talk to me about something, but due to my meeting, I couldn't talk to him, the next day he passed away. Upon learning about the wrecking news, not even a single tear rolled down my cheeks and from there, my life took a turn into depression. I mostly started staying silent, my BP started to shoot up and fear was all over me. I started thinking about what did my father want to talk to me about. That question imprinted itself on my mind and after that incident, I regularly started feeling giddy, my body used to shiver, my mind was full of unlimited thoughts, I started feeling feverish. I was then put on temporary medication. Again, after three months, my aunt's son also expired in an accident. From then my regular treatment started, my business got affected due to this. Earlier, I used to be a very happening person, full of confidence, talking in front of 1000s of people. But after those two episodes, my confidence plunged and started staying back at home. Sometime before my father's demise, my husband got a new opportunity. We both used to stay together 24/7 but due to that new opportunity, he stayed outmost of the time, working. Consequently, our communication got hampered, my husband's behavior changed towards me. He started talking bluntly with me. Meanwhile, my father came to know something about my husband and that was the reason behind his call that day. My husband had an extra material affair, which made our 18 years of marriage void and turned my life completely upside down. As a wife, I had unwavering faith in my husband but he broke my trust. He was in a four-year relationship, and I was not aware.

Even after those two wrenching incidents that took place in my life, my husband did not support me and chose the other relationship. That again got me in depression, a constant conflict took place and my home got disturbed, my BPstarted shooting and self-confidence started dipping. At times, I used to feel like giving up on life and ending it once and for all. I used to blame myself for all that had happened. I used to question myself as to what went wrong, where did I lack that my husband left my side. But then I used to think of my kids, what will happen to them if I commit suicide.

Some time back, I was related to a system where I used to motivate ladies but there I was, losing my self-confidence and self-esteem. I couldn't walk straight as I used to feel giddy most of the time. My husband gave me everything whatever I wanted but what he couldn't give was faith. He made a joke out of this relationship. Even with the treatment, I used to feel chocked. During those two to three years, there was not one single day when I did not cry. I couldn't focus on my kids nor could I focus on myself. I stopped going out, I felt like staying at home all the time.

One day, I went to my sister's place, as I reached there, I started feeling dizzy and I fell. My husband left me there went away. That was when my sister took me to Dr.Vaishalli and I met her for the very first time. She heard my entire case and started with homeopathic treatment. She also advised me to start with my healing treatment but due to some reason, it couldn't happen. I took medication for one month and returned home. I continued with her treatment and started feeling better. I felt that I will recover very fast. Then another treatment started; psychotherapy along with 40 days forgiveness and meditation session. In my counseling session, she told me to get over those emotions and be strong. She explained that betrayal is common nowadays; there are so many people who are experiencing this. After listening to her, I started working on myself and gradually got stable. I started taking initiative and attending the meditation, pranayam and the Wednesday session of meditation. I understood that the only person who can heal you is you yourself, medication is for a temporary purpose. I made my subconscious mind understand the fact that few things are not in our hands, what my husband did was his karma and I had forgiven him on the very day of realization. I had forgiven him for myself because if I would not have forgiven him, the problem would have multiplied and I couldn't have focused on my kids

I know that things cannot change in one night, but we have to keep going and keep the faith. Now, I meditate regularly, recite positive affirmations and do self-talk too. I have completely overpowered depression, today I am living a healthy and happy life with my kids, I am not on any medication. I would like to thank Dr.Vaishalli for transforming my life. One cannot always be dependent on medication, many times you have to take the initiative of coming out of these situations on your own. Reciting positive affirmations like I am healthy and happy helps the subconscious mind imprint and follow it.

CASE – 4

Being a mature and responsible girl of my family, I always thought of supporting them in all aspects of life, unaware of the consequences of my own decisions.

Like many others, my reason behind getting into depression was my love life, and the worst part of that I was not getting enough support from the person, for whom I invested so much of my valuable time.

Depression is a state in which a person gets hurt even with the slightest poke from another person, so one requires a lot of support, care and love from others.

Getting involved emotionally with the person to an extent led me to suicidal thoughts, but by God's grace, I came out of it.

Getting back to normal life would not have been an easy task without the love and support of my family. How could I destroy myself for a stranger when God has blessed me with a lovely family?

Suicide never takes the pain away.

NEVER DO SELF HARM. Feeling sad or moody sometimes is a part of life.

Those were the days I drew closer to my Creator. It was a completely different feeling knowing that the worldly life is just a delusion and this present life is a temporary thing for which we humans try to do so much. We take things for granted and are least bothered. The world will give you never-ending sorrows, but the remembrance of Allah is enough to enlighten your heavy heart and keeping the faith.

Reading Namaz and Qur'an became a part of my life. It strengthened me physically and emotionally and kept my faith intact. During the course, forgiveness and gratitude were of great help.

Moreover, homeopathy was what transpired the magic. My doctor cum my secret dairy Dr.Vaishalli helped me throughout all this, starting from counseling to being all ears to my day-to-day stuff. She gave her valuable time and advice and results started showing up. I just love to pour my heart out to her.

Thank you Dr.Vaishalli!

CASE – 5

Firstly, thanks to our Beloved teacher GMCKS for getting Pranic Healing in our lives.

I am Grateful to Dr.Vaishalli, our Pranic Healing Trainers and the one who introduced me to PH. While walking on the path of Pranic Healing, now it's a bit difficult to talk about being depressed. But If I time-travel myself to the past, this is what I recollect:

I was depressed right since my childhood; it might sound strange but it's true!

I belong to a very chaotic family. Father abusing mother, saw mother always yelling at father since he used to drink a lot. No one understood each other, no love, no affection, irritating siblings.

I always thought to myself; why am I around these people!

I always saw my mother being biased. Maybe as I was 2nd girl child, so the 1st daughter and the son got more priorities and I was left alone. I was always expected to do things whereas others got a levy. I always thought no one loves me.

As a kid when I saw some unfortunate people around, I use to feel their pain prominently as somewhere inside I was so much hurt.

I always felt like leaving the house but had lots of fear, where will I go, what will I do.

When I was 13, I started staying with my cousin and loved staying there, away from my family. There was so much peace and silence and hence I continued staying there during all my vacations until standard 12. But then I realized that I was always used as a servant of the house, made to do all the housework, hence stopped going there.

I always thought of options to escape from my family, so I again started staying with my cousins seeing so much love, care, bonding and discipline within their family.

My aunt suggested me to work, though frustratingly, I did and gave my salary to her. I continued to stay there like an upgraded maid again.

One day, I decided to go back to my family but seeing the havoc in my family, I took a step to finish myself because, at that point, I had realized that there was no reason for me to exist. Everyone took undue advantage of me and made me slog for a bit of peace!

I swallowed three strips of sleeping pills but God had a different plan for me, so today I am writing this. My aunt again offered me to stay with her, so I stayed with her, studied and also did the job. In the meantime, I got introduced to various meditation techniques but could not continue them, though I practiced whatever I learnt.

In 2017 I got introduced to Pranic Healing that helped me uplift myself from all the situations and circumstances.

After I got introduced to Pranic Healing, I completely understood that happiness or sadness is something that we create. And because we have these energies, we attract the same kind of people with identical energies. Hence, forgiving and blessing others not only helps them but also helps us as it comes back to us, giving inner peace.

It's in giving that we receive is what I always tell myself so if I share love, peace, that is what I am going to receive. I thank GMCKS for these priceless teachings. Now I embrace it–Kamini.

CASE – 6

One morning in February 2019, I suddenly felt a pinch through my heart, followed by severe pain, shortness of breath and sweating. The experience shook me to the core; angiography diagnosed that there were 85% clots in two very small blood vessels entering my heart. The vessels being very small, an angioplasty was out of the question. So, the doctors suggested that they would have to treat the clots purely with allopathic medicine and several health care measures.

My 8-day stay at the hospital was full of numerous suggestions from various doctors. The guidelines included items like:

1. Avoid excessive walking and exercise
2. Strictly do not climb stairs
3. Follow a very strict diet
4. Reduce weight
5. Maintain BP and Sugar levels
6. Strictly avoid any kind of stress

At first, all these instructions felt like I was stuck in a vicious circle. But I started following the doctor's instructions and tried to lead a normal life. Almost a year later when I went for my check-up my weight, BP and sugar levels came up to be exactly what I had left the hospital with. The doctor was very unhappy with the progress and the suggestion-parade continued.

By the time I reached home, I was very worried about my way of life. Even after following each instruction to the letter for almost a year, my status was still the same. I felt like I will never be able to lead a normal life again. That depressed me and obviously also impacted every-thing I did. My BP shot up, sugar levels fluctuated, sleep cycles messed up, I was enveloped in such melancholy that nothing felt worth doing. With the addition of the COVID19 situation and being stuck at home, my con-dition worsened. Fear occupied my mind and I had a constant feeling of being stuck in a deep dark well.

Almost as a last resort, I turned to God, Spirituality and Meditation. I started shifting my concentration from de-pressive negative thoughts to chanting mantras, recit-ing various stotras (holy odes), meditation sessions, ho-meopathic medicine and Pranic Healing treatment. The Pranic Healing treatment proved to be so amazing that I experienced an increase in my positivity in a single day! A feeling of hope emerged and I was able to push my-self towards visualizing my happy being. Within a week of Pranic treatment, I felt relaxed, calm and strong. It helped me get back my confidence and hope, and now everything I did, started having a positive impact on my life. I now continue to meditate, devote my time to spirituality and practice self-healing. Special thanks to Dr. Vaishalli for helping me make this paradigm shift in such less time - Gauri.

CASE – 7

I am Arvind, aged 49 years, with a height of 5 feet & 11 inches. I presently weigh 71 kgs and have never exceeded 76 kgs. The reason I am mentioning my height and weight is to give a clear picture that I have maintained good physical fitness.

I am a sales professional for the last 27 years and travel extensively (15 to 20 days) in a month. I did not have any regular schedule for my breakfast, lunch and dinner. Due to extensive traveling and staying away from home, eating out is a routine.

I am a very healthy person and I did not have any previous history of Blood pressure, Diabetes, Hypertension or any heart disease. However, my family medical history has not been good due to which I use to get my medical check-up done every year. My family doctor had prescribed me medication for a pre-diabetic condition.

On 11th Oct 2018, I had been to Nagpur for my regular official tour. The next day, that's on 12th Oct 2018, during my regular working at 12.30 pm I felt uneasiness and poking pain in my chest. That poking pain occurred 4 times in a span of 15 minutes but the duration of pain was for less time. I immediately visited the closest Doctor along with my colleague.

At the clinic the Doctor had my ECG done and asked for the previous ECG. I informed her that I am from Pune and the previous ECG was done by my regular doctor about one month back. She asked me for the ECG report which I arranged to show her.

The doctor checked the ECG and immediately gave me medication. She asked me to be at her clinic for the next two hours. She advised me not to travel on that same day. So, I came back to Pune the next day and visited my regular doctor. I underwent a complete medical check-up and was diagnosed with three blockages.

The Angiography was followed by Angioplasty on 26th Oct 2018. I recovered and was back to my normal routine after a week's rest. I resumed my regular touring and was feeling very confident regarding my health.

In the first week of Feb 2019, I again started feeling a little discomfort in my chest and visited my regular doctor. The doctor had all the required tests done (ECG, 2 D Echo and Stress test). The reports were normal and the doctor advised me to continue exercising and walking.

I continued with the prescribed medicines and my regular evening walks but the feeling of discomfort in the chest prevailed. Sometimes, the discomfort would escalate and I used to experience slight pain, which led to anxiety and sleepless nights.

I was visiting my regular doctor every month, complaining about the discomfort and slight pain but the doctor kept telling me to increase the level of exercise and continue walking.

The functioning of my heart was normal as per the ECG. The doctor kept instructing me that I needed to relax and carry on with the exercise regime.

In November, I visited an Ayurvedic treatment centre and had a very bad experience as the doctor there had a very negative opinion about my health condition.

My anxiety level and the fear within me surged. I started feeling that something worse is going to happen and desperately wanted to come out of it.

Then, I joined the Yoga classes of Dr.Vaishalli from 5th January and since then I have been doing yoga daily for one hour in the morning. My 6-km evening walk for one hour is also a regular routine.

I started feeling better and the frequency of discomfort and pain also reduced. Previously I used to have the feeling the discomfort every day and the pain also persisted throughout the day. Now, the feeling of discomfort had reduced and the pain was occasional (once or twice a week).

My anxiety level used to increase, which resulted in sleepless nights whenever there was discomfort and pain in the chest. I was telling myself that everything was ok as I did not have breathlessness nor I used to sweat. For the entire day, my mind was occupied with negative thoughts about my health and the problems my family would face in case anything worst would happen to me.

I discussed with Dr.Vaishalli and decided to start the treatment with her.

My first session was a very good experience. I was able to keep the negative thoughts about my health away and my mind was at peace. I continued with the healing sessions and homeopathy medicines. After the first five sessions, my confidence in my health was much positive.

The feeling of discomfort and pain reduced but the most significant benefit was that due to my increased confidence level about my health I was feeling very comfortable.

Presently I have completed two sets of five sessions of Pranic Healing and the other therapies with her. I am feeling more confident about my health. The feeling of discomfort and pain has certainly reduced. And even if it occurs, I am confident that everything will be normal, it is just a matter of time and I should not panic. The healing sessions have given me the strength to think positive

I am very much thankful to Dr.Vaishalli. I am continuing with the different therapies suggested by her and hoping that it gives me further strength to face and overcome my health problems.

CASE - 8

I, Vijaya, have been handling a small business in Mechanical Engineering for the last 30 years. Like the majority of people, I have treaded through a plethora of back-breaking challenges; life has been like a roller-coaster journey so far. In business, you have to consider all the aspects that affect a business like the client, finance, workers, suppliers and so many other things. Many a time, you get depressed, feel very low but you have to make up your mind to be strong and move on with a holistic approach to the situation.

In such challenging situations, we need to handle problems with a very cool head, balanced mind and thinking with a humanitarian approach. One has to go to the root of the problem and have sympathetic consideration about others. It is like tight-rope-walking and balancing at every moment.

You should not lose temper at all otherwise everything goes out of control including your health and even atmosphere in the family.

Over the years, Meditation has helped me a lot in coming out of such situations. Inculcating some hobbies and surrounding myself with good friends give a lot of peace to my mind. When I go through turmoil, to cool it, I turn to BHAGAVADGITA for my solutions. Lots of ritualistic behavior patterns which we were taught in our childhood are probably fading away like yoga, pranayama, prayers, faith, having gratitude in life, proper eating habits, etc. These have helped me in my depressive phases of life. Meditation, homeopathy and Bach flower remedies have helped me a lot in keeping me levelheaded, peaceful at the core of my heart and I feel this young generation should also follow it.

CASE 9

Jan 2019
We shifted to a new house; we all were very happy and excited about the new house.

For the first two months, I was very busy setting up the house. By March everything was settled but I was still busy as both of my daughters had their exams.

One day, my younger daughter came to me and told me something that scared me, I was completely shattered. She told me that she could feel something in her right breast. When we visited Dr.Vaishalli, she checked my daughter and told us that it was a cyst.

She gave my daughter homeopathy medicines, she also advised us to get a mammography done and see a specialist.

After the reports came, the specialist doctor prescribed medicines to my daughter and said that if the cyst grows faster, we will have to go for a biopsy. After this, we informed Dr.Vaishalli everything as I have great faith in her. She asked my daughter to continue homeopathy medicines and asked me to give my daughter healing as I had attended her Pranic Healing workshop. I was scared and depressed but always had faith in God, Dr.Vaishalli and Master Choa Kok Sui.

I started giving healing to my daughter, I healed her daily for some days. It was not very easy for me as it was on a very delicate part of the body. I was a little worried, then I started giving her blessings after my Twin Heart Meditation.

My daughter was also very disturbed and kept asking, "Why is this happening to me, mama?"

I told her too to keep faith in God, Dr.Vaishalli, Master Choa and Pranic Healing.

Eventually, the cyst size started to reduce and we made another visit for the mammography.

The specialist told us that the report was normal and within 3 months the cyst disappeared. Today my daughter is totally fine and I am happy.

I will always be thankful to Doctor Vaishalli for showing me the great path of Pranic Healing - Pradnya.

CHAPTER 6

THE RITUAL RECIPE

It is said that 'the proof of the pudding is in the eating'. You have to eat to find proof.

Integrity is very important in life. It helps significantly to move forward positively, hence you must develop it. Take action to experience the magic of the therapies with absolute involvement. Aim to change 1% daily and you will become the change. Build a proper circadian rhythm. Hope you know the Parkinson's Law – 'work expands so as to fill the time available for its completion'. So do not waste time to take action. Follow this recipe religiously for a month and start seeing the magic.

Start integrating these therapies and make these a part of your regime. For your convenience, I am now going to share the ritual recipe. You can use different variations for different days.

THE RITUAL DAILY RECIPE

- As soon as you open your eyes, say a gratitude prayer. Thank the Almighty for what he has given you

- Have a salt-water bath
- Exercise, yoga and pranayama
- Do meditation, affirmation and visualization of your goals
- Have the detox drink
- Stimulate your vagus nerve
- Plan out your day and follow it
- Wear a smile daily
- Humor is important, have a conscious hearty laugh at least 1-2 times in a day
- Follow the diet plan for breakfast, lunch and dinner abiding the same time daily
- Drink lots of water
- Before sleeping, think about your day. Forgive those who have hurt you so that the burden is released from your shoulders. Do journaling
- Keep fresh plants, flowers, water bodies, soothing music or mantras at home to have a lively and healthy environment
- Appreciate others and say thank you wherever required. The law says whatever you sow shall you reap. Appreciate yourself for the smallest achievement of the day.
- Check your emotional quotient daily.

You can have an accountability partner who helps you push to practice the rituals daily.

> **"You are not your habits.**
> **You can make or break your habits.**
> **Do not be a victim of conditions or conditioning.**
> **Write your own script, choose your own course, and control your own destiny."**
> **Stephen Covey**

If the need be, learn to say NO. Accept and love yourself. Many a time, you need to take actions even though you might not really understand how will it be. Bring down your goals to the next benchmark. Release your pressure. Stay where you are in. Don't worry about the future or what is coming next or how will you take action if something really comes in. The truth is, life is one big flow and by the end of the day, you should feel that you have done the best you could and track it. Your intentions are very important or are you ambiguous? Stop trying to be perfect all the time. You are the best right now, so start. The one who takes action might falter and make mistakes. It is better to make mistakes and move forward rather than just sitting at the fence, cribbing and waiting for someone to lift you. As the saying goes 'you can take the horse to the water but you cannot make him drink it' for him to drink, he has to make efforts. Don't worry about people, they may say what they have to anyways. So, get up and be the change as the change has to come from within. No one will bring the change for you other than you yourself. So, let's embark on this journey by healing and empowering ourselves.

CONCLUDING NOTE

If you want to get the most out of this book, do not let this DIY book gather dust on your shelf after you have read it. Walk your fingers and pick this book while you are relaxing on a Sunday morning or before you dive in bed after a tiring day. Randomly pick any technique and try to practice it or schedule to do it the next morning. Gradually, you will find the unwavering energy that will evaporate all the miseries in your life. You will find the gateway to live a life bursting with health (at all levels). Last but not least, you will unearth the wellspring of energy that will help you bounce back during the testing times and keep moving forward. Numerous people have been benefited by these procedures and they have been living a fulfilled life, so can you.

If you wish to share your experience after applying these practices or if you wish to attend my counseling session, here are my contact details:

EMAIL: dr_vaishalli@yahoo.in
WEBSITE: www.drvaishalli.com
FBPAGE: www.facebook.com/drvaishalli
LINKEDIN: https://www.linkedin.com/in/drvaishalli
TWITTER: https://twitter.com/DrVaishSpeaks
INSTAGRAM : https://instagram.com/dr_vaishalli

Wish you a happy, healthy and blessed life!

ACKNOWLEDGEMENT

Lots of gratitude to all those who have come forward to help me with my book.

Special thanks to my family, friends, coach, editor and all my patients without whom it would not have been possible.

THANK YOU

Thank You For Reading My Book!

I really appreciate all of your feedback, and I love hearing what you have to say.

I need your input to make the next version of this book and my future books even better.

Please leave me a helpful review on Amazon letting me know what you thought of the book.

Thank you so much!
Dr. Vaishalli Khangtey

www.ingramcontent.com/pod-product-compliance
Lightning Source LLC
Chambersburg PA
CBHW051428150726
48000CB00005B/2005